# PLAY BETTER
# HOCKEY

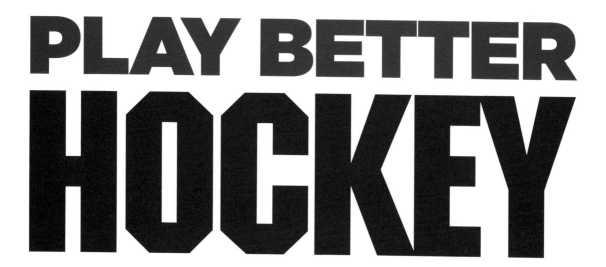

# PLAY BETTER HOCKEY

## Ron Davidson
## Foreword by Ken Hitchcock

**Second Edition
Revised and Expanded**

FIREFLY BOOKS

# A Firefly Book

Published by Firefly Books Ltd. 2017
Copyright © 2017 Firefly Books Ltd.
Text copyright © 2017 Ron Davidson
Images copyright as listed on page 159

First printing

Publisher Cataloging-in-Publication Data (U.S.)
Names: Davidson, Ron, 1957-, author.
Title: Play Better Hockey : The Essential Skills for Player Development / Ron Davidson.
Description: Richmond Hill, Ontario, Canada : Firefly Books, 2017. | Second Edition, revised, expanded. | Summary: "This book gives readers the tools they need to develop their hockey skills and master body position, skating and stick work"—Provided by publisher.
Identifiers: ISBN 978-1-77085-975-3 (paperback)
Subjects: LCSH: Hockey—Training. | BISAC: SPORTS & RECREATION / Hockey.
Classification: LCC GV848.3D38 | DDC 796.96207 – dc23

Library and Archives Canada Cataloguing in Publication
Davidson, Ron, 1957–, author.
  Play better hockey / Ron Davidson.—2nd edition, revised and expanded.
ISBN 978-1-77085-975-3 (softcover)
1. Hockey—Training. I. Title.
GV848.3.D38 2017   796.962'2   C2017-903261-5

Published in the United States by
Firefly Books (U.S.) Inc.
P.O. Box 1338, Ellicott Station
Buffalo, New York 14205

Published in Canada by
Firefly Books Ltd.
50 Staples Avenue, Unit 1
Richmond Hill, Ontario L4B 0A7

Cover and interior design: Gareth Lind

Printed in China

## Canadä

We acknowledge the financial support of the Government of Canada.

# Dedication

To my father, Al Davidson, who sadly passed away at the age of 91 the week this book went to press.

He received the Order of Canada in 2008 for a lifetime of promoting natural conservation in Canada, including his role in leading the creation of dozens of national parks, heritage sites and marine conservation areas. Somehow he still found the time to drive me to countless hockey games and practices, and took me to see the national team play when I was 10 years old. It was my dad that helped me to believe I could someday play for Canada, and he never missed a home game in my junior career or during my time with the national team—he even came on a road trip to Europe to watch me play. I am so grateful for everything he did for me.

Connor McDavid executes a high-speed lateral slide (see page 42) and reverse while handling a puck. McDavid's top hand is up and away from his body to keep his stick blade square to the ice, allowing him to control the puck. He will transition this slide into a tight turn on his backhand (see page 85).

# Contents

Chris Kreider transitions from a heel-to-heel turn (see page 88) to a v-start (see page 44) in order to reach a puck that has rebounded off of Jaroslav Halak.

# Foreword

I first met Ron Davidson toward the end of 2010. We were both hired to help run a special coaching and skills academy that would tour Canada over the winter of 2010–11. The academy was called Hyundai Hockey Nation and was run as part of *Hockey Night in Canada*'s greater hockey outreach programs. (Over the course of the 10-city tour, Ron and I worked with more than 6,000 players and hundreds of coaches.) Before the tour, I'd never heard of Ron. I learned shortly thereafter that he'd done camps for some NHL teams and that he was an enthusiastic teacher, but that was it. However, after one on-ice session at our first tour stop (Vancouver), I knew that in Ron, I was seeing something special.

Ron's role was to take drills that coaches like myself would devise and run the players through them. But Ron did more than just put the players through the paces; he emphasized which skills were being used and when, and he taught the players how to execute those skills in the same way that elite NHL players do. He would break down components of any given skill in a way that was easy to understand and follow (the drawings in this book are of Ron doing the skills). As a result, the players learned very quickly why their bodies needed to move through the skill in a certain way and how they could achieve that movement simply.

Ron's common-sense approach to skill development really impressed me. Ron was able to teach players in a way that had them executing basic to difficult skills in game-like situations right after having learned them. I've never met a coach who can explain a skill to a group of players and then excite the whole group so that each and every player wants to be the next great example that Ron can point to and say "this is how to do it right."

On the tour, Ron and I debated a lot about whether or not a player could be taught "hockey sense." Ron felt that he could produce a series of drills that could greatly enhance both players' skills and their sense of the game. Those are the drills highlighted at the end of this second edition. I wasn't convinced at first, but as our tour moved across Canada I saw that Ron was right. In one weekend I saw players elevate their senses and skills at the same time. Ron's approach to skill development, and his ability to include the skill in a competitive atmosphere that nurtured learning in a game-like situation, allowed a player's hockey sense to shine through (and be enhanced). I was, and still am, very impressed with the way Ron teaches. I now use some of his drills when coaching my own NHL team — and believe me, they work!

Ron's on-ice teaching and impact are expertly presented in this book, and if you want to take your game "to the next level," as Ron says, *Play Better Hockey* is a must read.

Yours in hockey,

Ken Hitchcock

Ken Hitchcock speaks to reporters in the spring of 2017 after being named the new head coach of the Dallas Stars.

# Introduction

I have loved this incredible game for as long as I can remember. With our skates already on, my brother and I would walk on the snow-covered road a few short blocks to the corner rink in Graham Park in Nepean, near Ottawa, Ontario, and spend hours playing. My dad tells me that there were many nights that he would come down to the rink, long after I was supposed to be home, and find me still wheeling around the ice. Sometimes I'd be by myself, sometimes with my brother, but I was always oblivious to the time. "You've got to come home," he would say, "before you freeze your toes off!"

In the winter of 1974, a few months before I was selected in the first round of the Quebec Major Junior Hockey League draft by the Cornwall Royals, my assistant coach in Midget, Tom Meeker, asked me what I was doing that summer and said, "My brother Howie runs a pretty good hockey school and he's looking for staff." During that first summer I discovered that I loved to teach hockey. Tom's invitation led to 12 summers of me working with one of the true masters of skill development—Howie Meeker was a great mentor. In my pursuit of an understanding of hockey technique, I couldn't have asked for a better beginning.

During those same years, I benefited from the instruction of some of Canada's best technical coaches: Brian Kilrea when I played for the Ottawa 67's in 1976–77, and Tom Watt, Clare Drake, George Kingston and Dave King when I played for Canada's National Team from 1978–83 (which included the Olympics in Lake Placid in 1980). When I played pro hockey for Vastra Frolunda in the Swedish Elite League, I was exposed to Swedish training programs. When I played pro in Switzerland, I had a Czechoslovakian coach.

I became a student of the game. I craved to learn as much as I could about how players developed hockey skills. Why do some players develop great glide while others don't? What is the secret to extreme speed on skates? Why does the puck seem to explode off of some player's sticks when they shoot and not others? I found that if I wanted the answers to these questions I needed to watch elite players and understand what they did to perform on the ice.

As a member of Canada's national team, I had the opportunity to play against some of the best players in the world. In 1978, when Father David Bauer was rekindling the program, which had been dormant for a decade, we played the Edmonton Oilers of the WHA, with their young star Wayne Gretzky. After playing against him, I realized that Wayne was

Ron Davidson (right) and Jim Nill celebrate a goal against Vladislav Tretiak and the Soviets in the 1980 Lake Placid Olympics.

totally unappreciated as a skater. His puck skills were incredible, but what really amazed me was his ability to move laterally, to accelerate through tight glide turns like no one else and to execute seamless transitions while always facing the play. Wayne was a true artist on skates and the ice was his canvas. He was able to move his feet and contact the ice to accomplish exactly what he wanted.

In 1980, I played in the Olympics in Lake Placid against some of the greatest Russian players in their prime, including Vladislav Tretiak, Viacheslav Fetisov and one of the most explosive players I have ever seen, Valeri Kharlamov. During games and practices, I had many opportunities to see their on-ice techniques firsthand.

On the heels of the 1972 Summit Series, the North American hockey community was beginning to realize that there was still a lot left to learn about the game. Before that famous series, the scouting report on the Soviets was that "they didn't even know which foot to shoot off," commenting on their tendency to shoot off their same foot. What no one realized then was how effective a shooting technique this was, allowing a player to shoot in motion and to release the puck with deception. In fact, what was forgotten was that two of the NHL's most dangerous scorers, Rocket Richard and Gordie Howe, had used the exact same technique. Now every elite player knows that he or she needs to have this ability in order to be successful.

The game continues to evolve, and it is the courage to question old ways of thought and the desire to be progressive in our approach to skill development that will allow the game to grow.

The greatest players in the game have always done this—and we need to follow their lead. I ran a clinic in Ottawa the day before the 2005 NHL draft to showcase the skills of the five players who were expected to be the top five picks in the draft, Sidney Crosby included. I designed a few drills to showcase his incredible acceleration and superb skating technique. What amazed me about Sidney was that even in a clinic that was essentially a media event, he was totally focused on getting the most out of the drills. He wanted to try new things, to push the envelope, to go even faster. The year before, Hayley Wickenheiser, one of the greatest female players in the world, was a guest instructor at one of my hockey schools for elite girls. Before long, she was jumping into the drills and trying the skating exercises. "I like the emphasis on quick transition and being light on your skates" she told me. "I could use that in my game!" It was obvious why she had reached the pinnacle of women's hockey. She never stopped learning.

Many elite athletes do not understand what they do technically that separates them from other players. Their hockey skills have become second nature. In 1981, Howie Meeker asked me to work with NHL players in order to instruct them on how to teach hockey to kids for the segment "Pro-Tips" for *Hockey Night in Canada*, and it was a real eye opener for me ... and for them! I outlined the skill progressions to Mark Messier, Denis Savard, Bobby Smith, Larry Robinson, Mike Bossy and others. The players were to then illustrate the skills on TV. Each player, without exception, indicated how helpful it was to break the skills down and that they would have benefited from the knowledge at an earlier age. They also said they would try to work it into their practices in the future. Thirty years later, from 2006–09, I was involved in coordinating the material for the skill segments show "Think Hockey" with Ron MacLean, which also aired on *Hockey Night in Canada*. I was the on-ice hockey director, and I worked with some of the NHL's top coaches and players including Ken Hitchcock, Mike Babcock, Wendel Clark and Larry Murphy — to present segments on individual and team skills and concepts important to the game. And while the game had certainly changed in three decades, the message remains the same: every player, regardless of age or ability, can improve their skills and can play better hockey.

There is no doubt that since our first edition of *Play Better Hockey* in 2010, hockey has continued to evolve at a rapid pace. Better training, coaching and equipment have all contributed to incredible progress in the individual and team skills of players. While grit, character, tenacity, willingness to compete and perseverance are intangibles that will always contribute to the success of elite players, there has become progressively more emphasis on skills. Speed and quickness have become paramount in the modern game. Parity and competition have motivated everyone involved in the game to pursue excellence in athletic performance.

It is so satisfying to realize that despite all of the changes in the game, all of the skills that we outlined in our first edition continue to be used by elite players today. The linear cross-overs used by Connor McDavid and others to generate extreme speed were described in detail in our first edition, as was the glide technique used by great skaters like Erik Karlsson and the tight turns and puck protection skills of Sydney Crosby — and they all appear in this book with striking photos of these amazing athletes. Glide continues to be as important as power to elite skating. Ankle extensions continue to be recognized as an important technique that players use to be even faster and quicker. They are all outlined in this book.

We are so excited about our second edition of *Play Better Hockey*. We have added lots of advanced skills, new photographs, some team skills as well as some of our top drills. The dynamic skill drills are flow drills that allow players to acquire and imprint essential hockey skills. These drills not only teach and test physical skills, they also teach and test mental skills — anticipation, the ability to read and react, vision and game sense. The drills are unpredictable, and they create tremendous activity. Players on the drill become "moving pylons" for the other players. Remember: players learn by doing. Keep them moving!

It doesn't matter whether I am teaching beginners or pros, young players or old-timers, girls or boys. The principles of technique and the skill progressions are the same. The difference in specific instruction depends on where the individual player is on the continuum of hockey development. As you strive to learn, your focus must be on the game itself: an incredible sport that demands an athlete to learn two extensions of the body — skates on the ice and a puck on the end of a stick. It is a combination of skating and puck skills, which, when coupled with vision and a sense for the game, culminates in the incredible athletic achievement we witness as hockey. And if acquiring a physical skill can be satisfying, then the network of skills that can be learned in hockey can offer untold enrichment. No matter your skill level, the better you get, the more you will enjoy everything hockey has to offer.

I sincerely hope this book helps you to connect to this beautiful game. There is no doubt that after reading this book and watching professional players use the techniques outlined within, you will come to a better understanding of how your body has to move to perform specific hockey skills. You will then be well on your way to achieving our goal for you—namely, to play better hockey!

# 1 Foundations

Sidney Crosby uses the perfect hockey-playing position (see page 16) while carrying the puck.

# Balance and Positioning

Developing great balance on skates is perhaps, athletically, the single most important building block to becoming an elite player.

You achieve balance through proper body position and a "flat blade." In the hockey-playing position and the hockey-skating position, your skate blades should be flat from front to back (weight evenly distributed over the balls and heels of your feet) and from side to side (equal pressure on the inside and outside edges of your blades). Whether with one hand on the stick or two hands on the stick, the hockey-skating and hockey-playing positions are the starting points from which all of your moves on the ice will be made.

**FIG. 1**

### Hockey-Playing Position (Side)

Your feet are parallel and shoulder width apart. Your knees are bent, and your back is straight with your body leaning forward. Your head is up and still. You are on a flat blade. Your stick blade is in front, square to the ice and between your shoulders toward your proper side, with your hands and arms out, away from your body.

**FIG. 2**

### Hockey-Playing Position (Front)

Bottom hand is in the center of your body and your top hand is in between the center of your body and your off-side hip. Your stick blade is flat on the ice and between your shoulders toward your proper side. Your feet are shoulder width apart pointing straight ahead.

**FIG. 3**

### Hockey-Skating Position

Your feet are parallel and shoulder width apart. Your knees are bent, and your back is straight with your body leaning forward. Your head is up and still. You are on a flat blade. Your stick blade is square to the ice in between your shoulders (toward your off side), and your top hand is away from your body in front of your off-side hip.

# Holding Your Stick

Learning to grip and hold your stick will allow you to always be ready to interact with the puck in any situation, whether you have one hand on your stick or two.

**FIG. 4**

### Proper Top-Hand Grip (Side)

When seen from the side, the butt end of the shaft should sit against the heel of your palm and your last two fingers should wrap tightly around the knob of the shaft. Your first two fingers and your thumb should grip the stick loosely. Your wrist should be relaxed and pointing slightly downward.

**FIG. 5**

### Proper Top-Hand Grip (Front)

When looking down on your hand, your thumb and forefinger should create a "V" that rests in the middle of the front of the shaft. Note that your thumb rests on the side of the shaft, not the top. Your thumb should not be applying any pressure to the shaft.

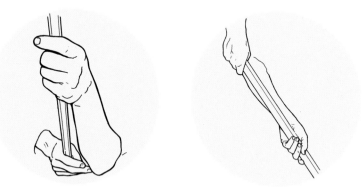

**FIG. 6 & 7 Bottom Hand Placement**

With your top hand in its proper position, place your bottom hand on the shaft by your top hand, and slide it down while keeping your forearm and elbow close to the shaft as you move your hand. Once the elbow of your bottom arm meets your top hand, lock your bottom hand here, as it is now in the proper position (for the hockey-playing position). Once established, move into the hockey-playing position, with your top hand close to the middle of and in front of your body.

## Top-Hand Grip

There is only one proper way to hold your hockey stick with your top hand. Proper grip is crucial to control the stick while skating and, ultimately, to control and handle the puck. It will also help you position your stick properly and, through that, help you to achieve proper body placement in all aspects of the game. It is best to learn the proper grip with your gloves off. Since it controls the stick, the top hand should be your dominant hand (for example, the right hand for a right handed person).

## Bottom-Hand Grip

Bottom hand placement and grip should change as play dictates. When you are handling the puck, your bottom hand should generally remain loose and flexible so you can easily move it up and down the shaft. Add firmness while puckhandling to help protect the puck from stick checks; apply even more grip when passing and more still when shooting.

You will often change the position of your bottom hand on the stick. Illustrated here is the ideal position for puckhandling when the puck is in front of you and in the middle of your body.

## Proper Arm Position

When puckhandling with two hands on your stick, you should line up your hands with the middle of your body and hold them out in front of you, placing your stick blade square on the ice. Your bottom hand should be in the center of your body and your top hand should be between the center of your body and your off-side hip.

It is crucial that you extend your arms out from your body enough so that, if viewed from the side, the elbow of your top hand does not jut out past your back, becoming visible behind you. If your elbow protrudes past your back when you handle the puck, you are either handling the puck too close to your body or your stick is too long.

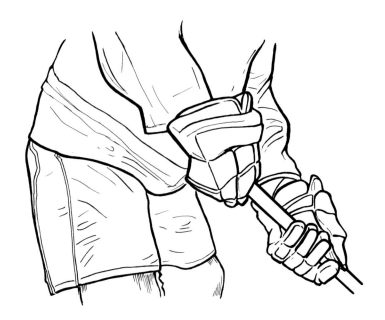

**FIG. 8 A Properly Held Stick**
Keep your arms out from your body and your stick blade square on the ice in the middle of your body. You will need to bend your knees and lean forward — key elements to your stance.

# Stick Selection

A hockey stick completes a hockey player. When combined with your skates and proper positioning, your stick becomes an invaluable tool and extension of your body. It serves to create the third pillar of a tripod (your legs — and skates — making the first two pillars), and it acts as a counterbalance. It also enables you to pass, shoot and score!

## Stick Size

Young players should not use a senior stick. The shaft and blade of the stick should be the right size for the player. Sticks range in size from youth to junior to intermediate to senior, and each has a progressively larger blade and bigger shaft (both circumference and length). If a stick with the proper size of shaft is not long enough for you, add a wooden plug to the shaft to extend the stick's length.

Ideally all players, particularly beginners, should use a stick that is no longer than half an inch below their chin when they are on skates and the stick is positioned upright with the toe of the blade touching the ice. Many elite players have sticks that are considerably shorter

**FIG. 9 Stick Lie**
The further your stick is from your body when gripped properly with your blade flat on the ice, the greater the angle of the blade will be in relation to the shaft. A hockey stick with a large lie angle (a) is referred to as a low lie, while a small lie (b) is a high lie.

than this. As you become more experienced, you can learn to handle the puck with a longer or shorter stick. Longer sticks have the advantage of more reach, while shorter sticks enable players to puckhandle much closer to their body while keeping their stick blade square to the ice.

## Stick Lie

Lie is the angle of the blade in relation to the shaft. Hockey sticks range from a low lie of 4.0 and move up in half increments to a high lie of 6.0. When you are using a stick with the proper lie for you, the blade is square to the ice when you are in the hockey-playing position. Players who carry the puck closer to their body will use a higher lie, while players who handle the puck away from their body will use a lower lie.

## Stiffness and Flexibility

Flexibility provides whip to your shots and passes, which contributes to the overall speed of the puck when fired from your stick. Composite shafts are all given a rating that tells you how flexible the stick is. The higher the number, the stiffer the stick will be. The flex number represents the amount of pressure (in pounds) it takes to bend the stick 1 inch (2.5 cm).

A good rule for players to follow when selecting a stick flex is to divide their weight by two. That number will give you a general idea of the flex you'll want in your stick. If you are very strong or take a lot of slapshots, you'll want to round up that number. If you take more wrist shots and snap shots, you may want to round down.

Having a stiff stick may result in more accurate shots, but they will be slower without the benefit of whip. Using a stick that is too stiff will cause the stick to recoil when shooting, because the shooter won't have adequate strength to keep the stick flexed during the shot. As a result, the stick will snap back before the shooter is done, creating a fluttering puck and an ineffective shot.

A flexible stick may result in faster shots, but they will be a little less accurate. Using a stick that is too flexible will cause the stick to flex too much, putting the shooter's hands too far out in front of the puck. As a result, the stick won't release the puck on time, creating a weak and loping shot.

Cutting a composite will impact flexibility. While it won't actually increase the stiffness of the stick (the material will stay as malleable as it was before you cut it), it will make the stick *feel* stiffer. That is because the length of the stick is shorter and there is less stick to flex. Less stick means less leverage and a firmer feeling stick. Many stick experts claim every 2 inches (5 cm) cut off the length requires adding 10 pounds (about 5 kg) of pressure to attain the pre-cut flex.

## Feeling the Puck

"Feel" is a player's sense of where the puck is on the stick and how the stick is moving the puck; feel is transferred through the stick to the player's hands. This sense, or message, from the puck to the player is clearest when transferred through wood, as opposed to composite. For that reason, all players, regardless of skill level, should consider a wooden plug at the top of the shaft of their stick (keeping in mind the need for a desired flex rating).

If you're learning to puckhandle or wish to improve your puckhandling, it is crucial that you select a stick you can handle easily and that maximizes your feel for the puck. Beginners should use a stick with a blade that is straight or has a slight and gradual curve and is as thin and flexible as possible. The thinner and more flexible the blade, the more feel of the puck it will transfer to its user.

# Skate Blades

A skate blade is thin and two-edged, made of stainless steel and mounted in a holder that is fastened with rivets to a skate boot. Each blade is contoured from toe to heel, which means that not all of your blade is on the ice at the same time. Each blade also has a concave groove running between the two edges, known as a hollow, which gives a skate an inside and an outside edge.

## Edges and Hollows

Edges provide control, and without them you would slip and slide. Having two edges with a hollow in between allows you to carve, draw or push off the ice with either the inside or outside of your blade, and it also allows you to glide. Glide is the direct result of the hollow's low level of friction as compared to the edges, which have a relatively high level of friction.

When you are coasting on the ice you are running on the edges of your blades and—depending on your weight, the pressure you apply and the ice conditions—the hollow of your blade. The deeper the hollow, the deeper the edges, and the more you will be running on your edges and the less you will be running on the hollow. This means more friction, which gives you more grip but less glide. The shallower the hollow, the more you are running on your hollow, which means less friction and more glide. Some friction is good, as it produces heat, which contributes to glide. Too much friction, however, impairs glide.

## Radius of Hollow

Radius of hollow (ROH) is the technical term to describe the depth of the hollow between a

A hockey skate boot, holder and blade make up a hockey skate. When the skate is sitting flat on its blade, as seen here, the blade radius (the contour of the blade from heel to toe) is clearly visible.

blade's edges. This measurement reflects the length of the radius of a circle, a portion of which forms the hollow between the edges: a small radius indicates a small circle and a deep hollow, while a large radius indicates a large circle and a shallow hollow. And so, a blade with a small ROH has a deep hollow that gives you less glide, but you will have more bite from your edges, enabling you to turn sharper and start more quickly. A blade with a large ROH gives you a shallower hollow, so the blade is closer to being flat between the edges, allowing you to glide better.

An ideal ROH will allow you to strike a balance between glide and

maneuverability. The key to finding your preferred ROH is to start at a relatively moderate ROH, such as ½ inch, and try increasing the ROH in increments of ¹⁄₁₆ inch. If you find that you want more bite and less glide, experiment by decreasing the ROH. When choosing an ROH, remember to take into account your ability, your playing style and your size, along with the ice conditions you are expecting—the ice NHLers play on is typically softer than your local rink or outdoor surface, and soft ice is friendlier to skate blades. The softer the ice, the more bite you will have, so it allows you to experiment with a higher ROH to improve your glide. Your weight is also an important factor. Heavier players will still have bite with higher ROHs. Lighter players may need lower ROHs because they need to increase the impact of their edges.

In terms of keeping your skate blade's edge, a deeper hollow exposes your edges more than a shallow hollow does, leading to a higher likelihood of nicks or burrs. Your skates will also become dull more quickly with a deep hollow. The shallower the hollow of the blade, the less likely it is to be compromised and the longer it will keep it's edge. This means that, typically, players with a deeper hollow should get their skates sharpened more often than players with a shallow hollow.

It should be noted that most players get their skates sharpened too often. You want to get your skates sharpened often enough for them to have consistent edges with consistent glide and bite. If your blades are protected off the ice and don't receive any nicks during the ice session—from contact with the goal post, other skates or sticks—they should remain consistently sharp for long periods of ice use, especially if you use a higher ROH.

When checking your blades,

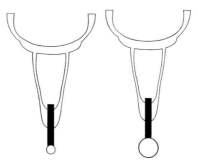

**FIG. 10 Radius of Hollow**
In these skate cutaways (in which you can see the boot, blade holder and blade — which is black), the ROH is represented by the circle at the bottom of the blade. The smaller circle represents a small ROH, while the larger circle represents a large ROH. The smaller the ROH, the deeper the hollow and the more edge you will have. The larger the ROH, the shallower the hollow and the more glide you will be able to generate.

make sure your edges are even. To check this, flip your skate over and place a dime on the blade so that it sits across both edges—if the skate is held straight the dime should be level. Even edges will allow you to glide on a side-to-side flat blade, meaning you will have equal pressure on both edges.

## Blade Radius

Player skates (as opposed to goalie skates) are often referred to as being "rockered," which means the blade is contoured, or not flat. The manufacturer does not preset contouring, and every new pair of skates has to be contoured before use. The technical term referring to the contour of the blade is blade radius, and this operates on the same principle as radius of hollow:

the measure of the radius is the measure of the circumference of a circle with a portion of that circle being the blade. Unlike radius of hollow, which is measured in inches, blade radius is measured in feet. The larger the radius, the less contoured the blade is and the more blade you will have in contact with the ice; the smaller the radius, the more contoured the blade is and the less blade you will have in contact with the ice. The more blade you have on the ice, the more impact your blade will have on your speed. Speed skaters, for example, use the longest blades possible while still allowing for quick starts and cross-over turns. The typical blade radius for a hockey player is 9 feet, but it can range from 6 to 13 feet. For goalies it is much higher since the blade is much flatter.

When deciding the radius for your skates, you should aim to have as large a radius as possible without sacrificing your maneuverability. As you gain experience, you can experiment with your blade radius and push toward a larger radius. Improving your skating technique, including your hand and body position, will allow you to be agile while using a larger blade radius. More importantly, using a large blade radius will offer you more glide (and more speed) in and out of turns and transitions. The radius for younger, smaller skaters will be shorter than for larger adult skaters simply because of the differences in the overall length of their

**FIG. 11 Blade Radius**
An example of a large blade radius. The flatter the contour (large blade radius), the more blade you have on the ice to contribute to glide, which will contribute to speed. With a smaller blade radius (rounder contour), you will have enhanced agility but will sacrifice some ability to glide.

**FIG. 12 Blade Pitch**
This skate is pitched forward, with the heel higher than the ball of the foot. Many skates are pitched forward, as the natural skating position is to be on a flat blade with a forward body lean.

## Skate Stones and Skate Sticks

Traditional flat skate stones can be used to keep your edges burr-free in between sharpenings. Skate sticks that are composed of a plastic handle and a ceramic Y, however, will distort your blade performance. The ceramic in the stick is stronger than the steel of your blade. Thus, when you run the ceramic Y over your blade, you are manipulating the steel of your blade edges. This action pushes the edges in a little, creating a similar edge-to-hollow ratio as if you were to have your skates sharpened with a deep hollow. Thus, if you apply too much pressure with your skate stick, you run the risk of ruining your ROH until the next time you get your skates sharpened.

blades. In any case, it is extremely important that the contour of your blade is centered. This will give you maximum balance, and it will allow you to apply equal force through the heels and balls of your feet when you thrust.

### The Relationship Between Radius of Hollow and Blade Radius

The relationship between blade radius and radius of hollow is where you can do your fine-tuning. For example, some players will use a large blade radius (for greater speed) combined with a small radius of hollow (for more bite for turning and starts), while other players will use a small blade radius (for better maneuverability) with a large radius of hollow (for better glide). Take your skill, technique, style of play and physical size into account when you choose the characteristics for your blades. Heavier players can take advantage of the increased glide of a large blade radius and may also find performance benefits from a large

ROH, as their weight will give their blades more bite, even with smaller edges. Lighter players can use a smaller ROH to get bite for turning and starting but may want a large blade radius to maximize their straightaway speed.

### Pitch of the Skate

The pitch of the skate is the angle of the foot relative to the blade on the ice, and it is determined by the position of the blade holder, which is attached to the bottom of the skate. Some blade holders are positioned so that your foot sits flat, while others are positioned so that your feet and the rest of your body naturally lean forward. Different makes of skates will have different pitches. The pitch can be changed by changing the blade holder or by inserting "lifts" to a portion of the skate's insole. Pitch is a matter of personal preference and does not depend on whether you play defense or forward.

When choosing the pitch of your skates, remember that the proper hockey-skating position is on a flat

Speed skates have a very large blade radius that allows as much blade as possible to be on the ice. With so much blade on the ice, speed skaters experience increased glide, which in turn increases speed.

blade with a forward body lean, whether you are skating forward or backward. It is also important to note that while you will thrust from both the balls and heels of your feet, it is quite often the balls of your feet that do the most thrusting. Therefore, a forward pitch is highly recommended. If you are skating with a forward pitch, be mindful not to glide only on the balls of your feet—maintain a good body position so that you skate on a flat blade with your weight evenly distributed between your heels and the balls of your feet.

## Debunking the Myths

At one time it was believed that the position you played should influence the characteristics of the blade you used. However, as technical instruction has progressed, it is now understood that all players, regardless of their position, need to be as quick, agile and maneuverable as possible and maintain maximum glide for speed. So there is no one-size-fits-all approach to blade style. Each player should be on the blade that works best for their individual needs, size and style.

# Body Terminology

Whether you are a righty or a lefty, every player has two sides to their body.

The two sides are delineated by the way you shoot. You have a forehand side (right for a right-handed shooter and left for a left-handed shooter) and a backhand side (left for a right-handed shooter and right for a left-handed shooter).

The forehand side is also called the proper side, and the backhand side is your off side. The forehand side (or proper side) is also often referred to as the "same side."

All of these terms are referenced throughout this book, as every movement you make on the ice and every shooting technique you'll execute will rely on understanding which side of your body you are using (or moving toward or away from) as you execute a given skill.

Proper side and off side are also used to describe a player's position in relation to the net. Players can be on their proper side when approaching the net (for example, a left-handed player on the left wing) or on their off side (for example, a left-handed player on the right wing).

**FIG. 13**

⊙ **Backhand side**

⊙ **Off side**

⊙ **Forehand side**

⊙ **Proper side**

⊙ **Same side**

### Shooting from the Same Foot

This shooter is a right-handed shot. He is taking a forehand shot by sweeping the puck from behind the heel of his same foot to in front of the toe of his same foot. With this mode of shooting, the shooter's weight is loaded to his same foot. This is called a "same-foot shot."

### Shooting from the Off Foot

This shooter is a right-handed shot. He is taking a forehand shot and by sweeping the puck from his same foot (his back foot in relation to his target) to his off foot (the front foot in relation to his target). With this mode of shooting, the shooter's weight is transfered from back to front (same foot to off foot).

# Skating Principles

Skating efficiently is the best and quickest way to improve your game. In order to become a better skater, you must embrace three important concepts: glide, drive and thrust.

## Glide

Glide is the ability to coast your blades along the ice with as little friction as possible. Glide turns power into speed. It also allows you to create momentum during transitions.

Every skating maneuver has an element of glide. While you are skating, the skate that is not driving is gliding, even if it is only doing so briefly. In some skating maneuvers, where both of your feet continually stay on the ice, such as when you are skating backward with both skates on the ice, you are gliding with both skates while you are driving (when going backward this way, the portion of the skate blade under the ball of your foot is thrusting while the portion of the skate blade under your heel is gliding).

The more efficient your glide, the less power you need to exert to skate quickly. Keep your glide skate flat and move your weight (hands, knees, etc.) over top and out in front of your glide skate. This will use your weight and momentum to generate glide. Executing a deep knee bend that is over the toe of your glide skate and moving your hands into the proper position ahead of your glide skate are two ways to use your weight to assist glide. A third is to load the weight of your body onto your glide skate. For example, when skating with both feet on the ice you can move quite quickly without actually "skating" simply by putting all of your weight on one skate and then transferring all of your weight onto

## Drills to Develop Single-Leg Balance and Maximize Glide

Throughout these drills, maintain the hockey-skating position and focus on promoting glide by keeping your knees bent — especially over your glide skate. You can use your stick to help maintain your balance by keeping its blade square on the ice and applying pressure through the shaft to the blade. This way your stick can act as a "third" leg.

### Toe Taps

In the hockey-skating position, pick up one of your feet and move it laterally, just above the ice, toward your other foot, and bring the insides of your skates together. Next, return your raised foot to its original position and then repeat with your other foot. As you become more comfortable, widen your step. Add puckhandling as you progress.

### Step, Glide and Touch (Toe Taps in Motion)

Take a forward lateral step (not a stride) away from your body and put your weight over your stepping skate; bend the knee of this skate and glide. Pick up your other skate, keeping it close to the ice, and bring it to meet your gliding skate. Tap your skates together and then take a forward lateral step with the skate you just picked up. Continue to alternate skates, making sure to tap your skates in between steps. As you progress, widen your step. Try the same drill going backward.

### Single-Leg Glide

Raise one skate off the ice and glide on your other skate. With your skate that is off the ice, execute leg and foot exercises. Alternate skates and try the drill both forward and backward. Here are a few exercise examples: you can rotate your hip and your ankle by pointing your toe out and in; you can move your skate away from your body and back toward your body; and you can bring your skate up and down while bending the knee of the skate you are gliding on to create a vertical weight transfer.

your other skate, each time bending the knee of the leg that is receiving the transfer of weight.

Remember, in order to glide your skates must be on the ice! The more your skates are in contact with the ice, the more efficient a skater you can be.

## Drive

Drive is one of two ways that you can develop power while skating. The leg and skate that are pushing against the ice to propel you is what accomplishes drive. As your drive skate pushes against the ice, it exerts force that is transferred to your glide skate (the skate that is not pushing). Remember, once you are moving, when one skate drives, the other glides. The harder you drive, the more energy you will direct to your glide skate. Provided you are gliding efficiently, a powerful drive will translate into speed.

## Thrust

Thrust is the second way to develop power while skating. Thrust is the additional power generated by the balls and the heels of your drive foot. When skating forward, for instance, extending and rotating the ankle of your drive skate, so that the blade beneath the

ball of your foot is pushed further into the ice, generates thrust. This ankle extension should occur at the same time as the extension of your drive leg so that the thrust happens just as you are set to complete the drive. Thrust, in other words, is a push you can add to the motion of your drive. When combined with the power of the initial drive, the additional surge of energy will increase the overall power available for your glide.

Great skaters can extend and rotate their ankles in almost any direction in order to generate the most thrust possible during any given skating maneuver. Timing is critical to maximize thrust

**Perfect Ankle Extension**

Taylor Hall concludes a picture perfect drive with a full leg extension by extending the ankle of his drive skate — pushing the blade beneath the ball of his foot further into the ice — for extra thrust. Hall enhances the speed transfered from his drive to his glide by using a deep knee bend, keeping his chest and shoulders square to his direction of travel. A forward body lean keeps his weight on top and slightly ahead of his glide skate, the blade of which is completely flat on the ice.

and, consequently, maximize speed. Proper timing of the thrust together with proper weight transfer is what is commonly referred to as "rhythm" in skating. Rhythm has a huge effect on a player's ability to skate efficiently and to generate momentum during skating transitions.

# ② Fundamentals

Erik Karlsson uses skating skills to win a foot race. He has two hands on his stick since he anticipates getting the puck. The entire blade of his drive skate is contacting the ice. Karlsson's shoulders and head are square to his line of travel, his back is straight and his body is leaning slightly forward. Ondrej Palat brings his upper body too far forward as he reaches for the puck. Unlike Karlsson, his weight is not over his drive and glide skates, reducing his speed at a crucial moment.

# Forward Stride

You must be able to move forward in a straight line as fast as possible, with or without the puck. There are many game situations when straightaway speed without the puck is important: when racing for a loose puck, when chasing an opponent, when forechecking, when backchecking or when trying to get open for a pass. The fastest and most efficient way to move forward is by using the forward stride, striding (driving) with one leg and then the other, over and over. When one leg is striding, the other is gliding.

## The Motion of the Drive Skate

Start in the hockey-skating position. With both skates parallel and under the center of your body, point your feet straight ahead. Make sure that the blades of both of your skates are flat, which will allow maximum glide on the glide skate and maximum push off the drive skate. With a deep knee bend, begin to rotate the toe of your drive skate out and away from your body. At the same time, push the entire inside edge of the blade of your drive skate into the ice and away from your glide skate. Do this using both the ball and the heel of your drive foot to produce a uniform push across the entire blade. The glide skate will move forward while you push the drive skate on the ice and extend your drive leg. When you push, you are rotating (opening) your hip and knee as you extend and straighten your leg. You need to rotate your hip and knee enough so that the angle of the drive skate relative to your line of travel increases progressively, reaching a maximum of 90 degrees to your direction of travel at the end of your stride.

Remember that as you drive, you are not only directing a surge of

power toward your glide skate, you are also transferring your weight to the glide skate. At the start of a stride there is an initial transfer of weight to the glide skate, and more weight is progressively transferred to the glide skate as the stride continues. Transferring body weight to your glide skate, coupled with a balanced glide leg, allows you to be in the proper linear body position throughout your stride—your weight over your knee which is over the ball of your glide foot.

## The Thrust of the Drive Skate

At the end of your stride, when your leg is *almost* fully extended and your drive skate is 90 degrees to your line of travel, push off the ice. Start the push using your full blade and end the push by extending your ankle down into the ice, away from your body. The extension will give you an added thrust to your stride.

Your ankle extension and final thrust should be off the inside edge of the ball of your foot. Remember to extend your leg completely as you finish your thrust.

## Body Position Throughout the Stride

Throughout the stride, keep your head and torso as still as possible. Keep your shoulders square to your line of travel and your back straight as you lean your body forward. At all times, your glide skate should remain in a straight line and on a flat blade in line with your direction of travel. Use a deep knee bend to keep your body weight forward, over your glide skate. The knee of your glide leg and the hand of your glide arm should be over the toe of your glide skate. Your glide-side arm should swing forward (but not across your body) as you drive.

Being in the proper body position throughout your stride allows you

to use the large muscle groups in your body, such as your back and quadriceps, to increase the strength of your drive throughout your stride.

## Recovery of the Drive Leg

After you make the final thrust off the ball of your drive foot, you must bring it back (recover) to the glide position, as your glide foot will then become your drive foot. You must do this as quickly as possible so your other skate can begin to stride and thus keep you moving forward as quickly as possible. The speed of your recovery is crucial to executing the most strides in the shortest amount of time. Recover as quickly as possible by fully transferring your weight to your glide skate during the drive motion. As well, keep your drive skate up off the ice, but as close to the ice as possible, after the final thrust and during the recovery. Your single-leg balance is extremely important throughout the stride, as it allows you to fully transfer your weight, which enables maximum glide and drive for the quickest recovery.

## The Cycle of Power

Once you recover your drive foot and drive with your glide foot you will have completed one full drive cycle. Repeat the entire process until you have reached your goal, whether it be catching a player or breaking for open ice.

# Left Leg Drive, Right Leg Recovery

**1** Connor McDavid is starting to drive with a uniform push across the entire blade of his left skate. As he continues the drive, he will rotate his skate out to a 90-degree angle from his direction of travel. At the end of the drive he will thrust from the ball of his foot and increase his speed by extending his ankle down, forcing his blade further into the ice.

**2** McDavid's right skate is recovering from the drive. He will keep his recovering skate low to the ice so he can get it in a gliding position as soon as possible.

**3** McDavid's shoulders and chest are square to his direction of travel. His head is up and looking at his target, his back is straight and his body is leaning forward. McDavid has one hand (right hand) on his stick. This hand will drive forward, with the stride of his left leg. His stick blade is square to the ice and between his shoulders.

**FIG. 14 Start**
Feet underneath your body on flat blades increases the weight you can contribute to your drive.

**FIG. 15 Initial Push**
Initial drive foot is turned out to begin your stride and knees are bent to power your drive. Push uniformly across the entire blade.

**FIG. 16 Drive**
Continue the uniform push across the entire blade while you shift to using your inside edge exclusively, while at the same time rocking from your heel to the ball of your foot for the final thrust.

## Tips for Speed

Proper positioning and good conditioning of your quads, hamstrings and core will help you attain speed, as will the following tips:

✳ Skate efficiently: keep your head and torso still and your shoulders square.

✳ Glide is as important as power. Glide on a flat blade and with a deep knee bend.

✳ If there is no immediate chance

### Perfect Glide
Erik Karlsson has finished thrusting with his right skate and is gliding beautifully on his left skate. The key to Karlsson's glide is a flat blade (efficient transfer of drive power) and a good knee bend with body weight slightly over and ahead of his glide skate (weight increases glide). Keeping square to his direction of travel with his glide skate pointing straight makes him a more efficient skater.

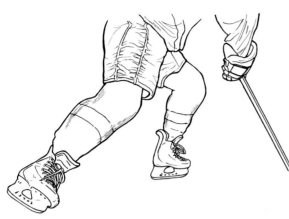

**FIG. 17 Thrust**

**From the ball of your foot, push hard down into the ice. For extra speed extend your ankle down and away from your direction of travel, forcing your blade into the ice.**

**FIG. 18 Glide to Stride**

**Throughout the entire stride (Fig. 14–17), keep your glide foot flat with your weight ahead of your blade to keep you traveling straight. As your drive foot recovers, begin striding with your glide foot — progressively rotating it out 90 degrees from your direction of travel — to set up your drive.**

of getting the puck while striding, only your top hand should be on your stick.

✳ If you are looking for a pass or are about to enter a battle for the puck, both of your hands should be on your stick. Do not move your hands and stick side to side; rather, move them back to front in sequence with your stride. Do not let your arms cross the centerline of your body.

✳ Keep the blade of your stick square to the ice and between your shoulders.

## The Secret to Going Even Faster

You can add another gear to your forward stride by extending your ankle at the end of each stride. When your drive leg is almost fully extended, with the heel of your skate blade still on the ice and

your foot 90 degrees to your line of travel, push down and off the ice using your heel. Next, rock on your drive skate blade from your heel to the ball of your foot, and at the same time extend your ankle down and away from your line of travel. This drives the ball of your foot down into the ice and creates thrust, which will propel you quickly forward. Rocking from the heel to the ball of the foot is much the same technique basketball players and high jumpers use to spring up and sprinters use to run fast. The heel rocking to the ball of the foot coupled with the increased push off the ball of the foot by extending the ankle greatly increases the force of the final push at the end of each stride.

## Notes

If your arm crosses your centerline at the end of your stride, it will force the heel of your skate off the ice, and you will not be able to use it to push and rock onto the ball of your foot. This will considerably reduce the thrust you will be able to generate. Also, players who skate with both hands on their stick and move their hands laterally across their body are not able to use an ankle extension effectively; remember to move your hands in sequence with your stride, back to front. Finally, it takes great single-leg balance and timing to complete an ankle extension and not reduce the speed of your drive leg's recovery. It is rare for younger players to be able to master this technique, but mastering it can give you an edge over an opponent on a straightaway. It is very important that your skates are flexible enough to allow you to extend your ankles.

# Forward Glide

## Two-Foot Glide

**1** Claude Giroux is moving forward with a two-foot glide. His weight is loaded on his same side, meaning his same foot is the primary glide skate. With his stick controlling the puck on his forehand side, Giroux is well set up to drive with his off foot or to pass or shoot. He is opening up his body to increase his area of vision.

**2** While gliding, Giroux's off foot is also acting as his drive skate. His off-foot skate is not perfectly flat side to side, and the pressure he is applying to the inside edge of the blade of his off foot allows him to drive while keeping his weight over his gliding foot. This allows him to increase his speed while gliding on two feet.

**3** Giroux's knees are bent, allowing him to easily rock side to side as he laterally transfers his weight from one leg to the other.

You need to be able to generate forward speed with both of your skates on the ice. Defensively, when containing and possibly contacting a player, having both skates on the ice allows you to maintain your body position while angling toward the offensive player, and it gives you stability just before contact. Offensively, if you are in a good position but want to move forward, such as when you are trailing a play or are in the high slot and in a good shooting position, you will want to generate forward speed while gliding.

## Beginning to Glide

To glide efficiently (from a position where you are already moving or a standing start), equally distribute your weight over your heels and the balls of your feet and ensure your blade is flat. To generate extra speed in this position, transfer your weight back and forth, completely over one skate and then over the other. This is a lateral (or horizontal) weight transfer. Moving your body weight up and down by bending and straightening your knees (vertical weight transfer) will also add speed.

In this position you can "stride" by alternately bringing one skate underneath you, touching it to your other skate and then pushing it in a stride motion away from your body with a full leg extension before recovering it back underneath you. Always keep your skates on the ice and always stay on a flat blade on your glide skate while executing this stride.

## The Power of the Heel Push

When you are moving forward with both skates on the ice, you can achieve maximum speed by generating thrust with a heel push: driving the inside edge of the heel of your skate into the ice and away from your body while gliding on a flat blade (this looks like a half-moon, or the letter "C"). The strength of your heel push will depend on the level of acceleration you require. The timing of your

heel push is also critical. You must push when your drive skate is underneath you, or close to that position, ensuring that your body weight is over your drive skate at the time of your thrust.

Remember to drive with the heel of your drive skate while continuing to glide with a flat blade on the ball of your foot on your drive skate (while at the same time gliding on your other skate). If you put too much weight on your heels you will decrease your glide.

## Heel Push Drill

The goal of this drill is to skate circles around a stick lying on the ice by only using heel pushes and gliding. To start, lay your stick on the ice and enter the hockey-skating position with your skates together and parallel to your stick. Turn the toe of your outside skate out 90 degrees. This is your drive skate. While always keeping your drive skate on the ice, drive forward by pushing the inside edge of your heel into the ice. Continue to extend the leg of your drive foot away from your inside skate (your glide skate). Recover by bringing your drive skate back underneath you to touch your glide skate, and remember to keep both skates on the ice at all times. Repeat the drive and ensure that you glide on a flat blade with both skates while you push.

**FIG. 19**

**Heel Push Extension and Recovery**
Your drive leg is fully extended with your blade flat, front to back, when you end your drive. Keep your glide skate in a straight line underneath your body throughout the entire heel push and extension. This will maximize your glide and help you to avoid "weaving" back and fourth.

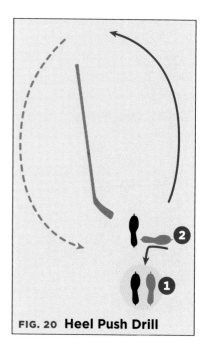

**FIG. 20 Heel Push Drill**

# Forward Cross-Overs and Cross-Unders

You can generate a lot of forward speed by using cross-overs with cross-unders while driving forward and laterally with both skates. You can use this technique from a stationary start; when moving forward in a turn or circle that is not tight, such as when driving to the net; when accelerating out of a tight turn; and when moving forward and laterally up the ice on an angle. Players like Connor McDavid use linear cross-overs throughout their forward skating to generate extreme speed.

## Drive with Both Skates

To start the cross-over motion, thrust from the inside edge of your outside skate at the ball of your foot as you pick this skate up to cross it over your inside skate. Quickly follow this with a cross-under: rotate the ankle of your inside skate and thrust underneath your cross-over skate from the outside edge of your blade at the pad of your foot. Extend your ankle (as your leg reaches the end of its drive) to drive the pad of your foot down into the ice to generate more thrust.

When doing cross-overs, emphasize the drive with short, quick strokes. Extend each of your legs at the end of their drives (especially when coming out of a turn).

The lower your skates stay to the ice throughout the cross-over, the quicker your recovery, the stronger your drive and the more time your blades will be on the ice to thrust. With cross-overs you want both skates to be driving at all times, and you want to move your skates so they cross closely together underneath you. This allows you to

## Crossing Over to Crossing Under

**1** Connor McDavid generates speed with a linear cross-over to his backhand side. He keeps his cross-over skate (outside skate) very close to the ice while crossing over top of his inside skate, which allows for an efficient, quick recovery and speedy repetition of his stride.

**2** McDavid's cross-under skate (inside skate) is nearly finished driving underneath the cross-over skate. He is thrusting from the outside edge of his blade, using the ball of his foot while extending his ankle and driving the ball of his foot down further into the ice.

**3** McDavid is bending his knees, allowing him to vertically transfer his weight into the cross-over and cross-under, maximizing his drive and ensuring as much blade as possible is on the ice for his cross-over and cross-under thrust.

**4** McDavid is moving his top hand into his body (but out from his hip) and pointing his head up toward his line of travel. As he continues on the trajectory of his turn, his shoulders and chest will come square to his direction of travel and his stick blade will be between his shoulders.

**FIG. 21 Crossing Over**

Lean into your turn and push off of the ice with the inside edge of your cross-over skate at the ball of your foot. Keep it as close as possible to the ice and the skate you are crossing over.

**FIG. 22 Crossing Under**

As your outside skate is crossing over, rotate your ankle on your inside skate so that you are using the outside edge of that skate, and push, with the pad of your foot, underneath the skate that is crossing over. Recover this foot quickly toward the center of the turn so that you can cross under again.

use as much of your body weight as possible to assist your thrust.

### Rhythm Adds Speed

You will generate more speed with your cross-overs when you vertically transfer your weight by bending your knees in rhythm with your drive and leg extension. This is because bending your knees adds body weight to your drive and allows you to get more of your skate blades on the ice, increasing your thrust; players call this "bounce." The key to bounce is to vertically transfer your weight but still keep your skates on or close to the ice.

### Stick Position

Where you put your stick always dictates the position of your hands and body; cross-overs are no different. The blade of your stick should always be between your shoulders, which should be square to your line of travel. Therefore, if you are doing cross-overs around a circle on the ice, you are looking into the circle but the blade of your stick should be on the circle itself and in front of you, *not* pointed toward the face-off dot. To place the blade of your stick in this position when crossing over to your backhand, move your top hand away from your body. When crossing over to your forehand, move your top hand into, and possibly across, your body. This will add glide and speed to your cross-overs and will help you protect the puck. Both of these positions are very similar to the positions you use when doing tight turns (see page 84).

# Backward Stride

All players must be able to skate backward with balance and speed. If you are playing defense and can match the speed of attacking forwards when skating backward, you can maintain proper positioning. Forwards often skate backward during a game, especially when moving into the proper shooting position, when assuming a proper position while forechecking or when defending after replacing a pinching player on defense. The skating principles that apply to the forward glide (see page 34) also apply to the backward stride. The exception is that your thrust now comes from the balls of your feet as opposed to your heels.

### The Drive

Start in the hockey-skating position with your feet together and parallel. Make sure to keep a deep knee bend and your back straight with your heels down on the ice. Turn the toe of one of your feet inward, this will be the foot you first drive off. Thrust yourself backward with your turned foot, from the inside edge of your blade at the ball of that foot. This stride is like the stride of the heel push (only backward—see page 35) and should create a half-moon or the letter "C." Put as much pressure as possible onto the ball of your foot for the drive, particularly at the start of your stride.

### The Stride

After your drive, continue to extend your stride leg fully out in front of you. However, you'll notice that the slower you are traveling the wider your stride will be. As you travel faster the thrusts from the balls of your feet will become straighter and less out and away from your body. Be sure to keep your glide leg traveling in a straight line underneath you, with the heel of your glide foot down. This allows you to take advantage of your weight, which will help you promote glide. At the end of your stroke, recover your stride foot and bring it back underneath you, beside and touching your glide foot. This is called "push and touch." It ensures that you get a full stride and that, before your glide foot begins its stride, your drive foot has come back and is ready to glide. In the backward stride, both skates stay on the ice at all times. You can use vertical and horizontal transfers of weight, just as you would use during the forward glide and forward stride.

### Notes

It is important to focus all of your power on moving backward as fast as possible in a straight line. When your drive skate is going through the stride motion, your glide skate must be in a straight line under you

**FIG. 23** **The Drive**

Toe is turned inward and your blade is flat on the ice. Push backward from the inside edge of your blade at the ball of your drive foot. Do not pick up your heel: your push should be a full-blade thrust with emphasis on the ball of your foot. By keeping your heel on the ice you are gliding on your heel while you are thrusting, making you go faster.

## Backward Stride and Glide

**1** Nathan Beaulieu's head is up and his shoulders are square, opposite to his direction of travel; his back is straight with a forward lean.

**2** His hands are in the hockey-skating position. The knee of his glide leg is well bent to keep his weight over his glide skate for better glide and stability.

**3** His glide skate is traveling straight and on a flat blade for the most efficient glide.

**4** His striding leg is mid-stride, with the heel and ball of the foot still in contact with the ice. Beaulieu uses a "C" cut to start his stride and then keeps the heel of his drive skate on the ice while applying downward pressure with the ball of his foot through an ankle extension.

**FIG. 24 End of the Stride**

Continue your initial push by extending your drive skate (with a flat blade) out in front of your body. For added speed before you recover your stride leg, extend your ankle forward at the end of your stride and thrust the ball of your foot into the ice. Use the rocking method you learned in the forward stride (see page 30). Pumping your arm and pointing it in tandem with your striding leg will increase your speed.

and your shoulders must be square, so that you are facing opposite your direction of travel. This ensures that you will move straight backward rather than turning from side to side with every stride.

The most common mistake players make when striding backward is lifting their heels off the ice. This action makes you lose the crucial heel glide that promotes speed and keeps you headed straight backward. Other common mistakes are not extending the drive leg fully, which maximizes thrust, and not bringing the feet together underneath the body between strides, which maximizes the body weight on the glide.

## The Secret to Extreme Speed on a Backward Stride

If you want to maximize your backward speed, you must learn to extend your ankles to create thrust. Start flexing your ankle when your feet are together, at the start of your stride. This ankle extension will continue through to the end of the stride. At the start of each stride, the pressure should be down and out through the ball of your foot, opposite your direction of travel. This push is commonly called a "C" cut. However, as you gain speed the thrusts from the balls of your feet will become straighter and less out and away from your body. The key to maximizing the thrust from the ball of your foot is to extend your ankle down into the ice and push back away from your body opposite to your direction of travel.

# Backward Cross-Under

The ability to turn is important whether you are skating forward or backward. Performing a backward cross-under allows you to accelerate while turning backward, which can help you get into a proper defensive position quickly and, offensively, get open for shots and passes. You can use the cross-under technique during many other skating maneuvers, such as backward skating, backward lateral skating and transition skating, to add speed and acceleration to your game.

## Backward Lateral Skating with a Cross-Under

**1** Colton Parayko is using a backward cross-under to move laterally and stay square to the attacking forward. His head is up and looking at the attacker. His shoulders are square, and his back is straight with a forward body lean. The blade of his stick is on the ice and between his shoulders.

**2** To maximize the thrust of his cross-under skate, Parayko is rotating his ankle to use the full outside edge of the blade on the ice. He generates thrust laterally and backward by extending his ankle and driving the ball of his foot into the ice.

**3** The thrust from his cross-under skate will move Parayko to his right. To continue moving in this direction, he will reach his cross-under skate laterally to his right as it recovers, plant it and then "pull" the ice toward him while executing another cross-under stride and thrust with his right skate.

**4** As Parayko's left foot hits the ice it will become his glide skate, sending him backward. Keeping this skate on the ice gives Parayko speed and stability.

## Not a Cross-Over

This technique is not a cross-over—it is a cross-under. Contrary to the commonly held view, and unlike when turning forward, you cross your feet under, not over, when turning backward. With cross-unders, your glide skate (outside skate) stays on the ice at all times to maximize glide and stability. Even your driving skate stays close to the ice, since you don't need to pick it up and move it over your gliding skate, making this a very efficient skating maneuver.

## Setting Up

As you are skating backward in the hockey-skating position, lean your body in toward the inside of the turn you wish to take. Keep your shoulders square and turn your head toward the inside of the turn so you can see where you are going. If you have the puck, or it is in immediate play, skate with two hands on your stick. Otherwise, skate with only your top hand on your stick.

## Reach and Pull

Your inside skate should drive and do all of the work. Your outside skate should glide and provide stability. Begin the cross-under stride by reaching your inside skate into the turn, away from your body, and "grabbing" the ice with the full length of the blade. Next, "pull" the ice you just grabbed toward you with the inside edge of your inside skate.

**FIG. 25 Cross-Under**
**Glide skate remains flat while your drive skate crosses underneath and behind the heel of your glide skate. Finish the drive with a thrust from the outside edge of your skate blade at the ball of your foot. For extra power extend your ankle down, forcing your blade into the ice.**

This is commonly referred to as "reach and pull."

## Push and Thrust

As your inside skate pulls progressively closer to your outside skate, you need to cross it underneath your body and behind the heel of your outside skate to push and thrust, completing the stride. To do this, bend the knee of your inside leg progressively so the full blade of your inside skate can remain on the ice to push. As well, rotate your inside ankle so, as your blade drives underneath you and behind the heel of your outside skate, your skate will transition from the inside edge to horizontally flat then to the outside edge.

As you cross your inside skate under you, you should be pushing with the outside edge of your blade. As you continue to push past the heel of your glide skate you will need to extend your leg and thrust. Use the pad of your foot to propel the thrust at the end of your drive and extend your ankle to maximize this thrust.

## Recovery

Right after the final thrust, start your recovery by quickly moving your drive skate back to a position where it can "reach and pull" again. You are stepping with your skate toward the inside of the turn. When recovering, try to keep your drive skate as close as you can to the ice. Remember, you are repeating the stride with the same leg (the inside leg).

## The Glide Skate

Your outside skate (your glide skate) remains on the ice at all times throughout the reach and pull, the push and thrust and the recovery. To maximize the glide on this skate, make sure you stay on a flat blade. Proper body position will ensure that your weight is evenly distributed on this skate and you are on a flat blade. Both your drive leg (your inside leg) and glide leg (your outside leg) require a deep knee bend; this promotes glide as well as balance and drive. Your glide skate must glide efficiently in order for you to maximize the acceleration you have while turning backward.

# Lateral Slides and Stopping

Every player needs to be able to stop, but it is not often that you will come to a complete stop during a game. Sometimes you will want to go to a certain place on the ice and stay there temporarily. Other times stopping is the most efficient way for you to reverse your direction, and you may need to stop if you have limited room to maneuver.

a very brief moment, such as in a forward-to-forward transition (see page 80), and other times the slide is more pronounced, such as a two-foot stop. The hardest skill to learn is how to do a lateral slide over a longer distance without stopping, with knees bent and ready to drive.

## The Lateral Slide

The lateral slide is a technique that not only precedes a stop, it is also used during some transitions—such as going forward to backward and going forward to forward—in order to preserve speed. You can also use it as a technique on its own to move laterally with or without the puck.

A lateral slide is preformed anytime both your feet are turned 90 degrees to your direction of travel while your momentum carries you in your original direction. Sometimes this is for

Begin a lateral slide by transitioning from a forward glide (having both of your feet coasting parallel on the ice with your toes pointing in the direction you are traveling in) to having both your feet and your body turned

90 degrees to your direction of travel. To do this, straighten your legs to lift your weight off your skates and exit the forward glide; the decreased pressure on your blades allows you to turn both your feet and your body against your direction of travel. Once turned do not apply any pressure on your skates, as this will make you stop. Instead, keep your legs straight and continue being light on your blades. It is important that both skate blades remain flat.

The less pressure you put on your blades, the less resistance you'll encounter and the more you will slide. You will eventually stop when the pressure of your blades causes enough drag to bring your lateral slide to an end. On a fresh sheet of ice, a proper lateral slide will leave two parallel scrape marks that look like jet streams and that end together at the center of your back skate's blade. As you become more adept at sliding laterally, practice bending your knees (vertical weight transfers) while

you slide. A bent-knee lateral slide is the best way to accelerate out of a transition, as your legs must be bent at the end of your slide to maximize your initial drive.

## Two-Foot Stop

Stopping on two skates requires a lateral slide on both blades with a gradual application of pressure until the drag created by the blades on the ice makes you stop.

Start the stop motion from a forward glide and transfer to a lateral slide with both of your feet. Once in the slide, put your body weight onto your skates by bending your knees (vertical weight transfer). The deeper you bend your knees, the more pressure you apply to your blades; the quicker you bend your knees, the quicker that pressure is applied. This allows you to control when and where the stop is made. As your stop advances, lean further away from your direction of travel and increase the pressure on the inside edge of your front skate and the

outside edge of your back skate.

You will need speed to do this adequately. Remember to keep your skates close together in the slide to effectively use your edges when you stop. As you continue to practice you'll get more comfortable using the outside edge of your back skate. You should progress to the point where you are executing two-foot stops with your feet almost touching.

As you master the lateral slide, you will be able to determine how long to glide before rotating your body and how long to slide laterally before stopping. The glide can be very short as the transition from skating to stopping can be very quick.

You can also perform a two-foot stop without rotating your upper body. Instead, keep your shoulders square to your direction of travel by only turning from the waist down when stopping. You'll want to stop this way to keep facing the play, especially if you are looking for a pass or a rebound.

## Two-Foot Stop

**1** Claude Giroux is leaning his body away from his direction of travel to increase pressure on the inside edge of his off foot and the outside edge of his same foot, turning a lateral slide into a two-foot stop; his shoulders and head remain square to the direction his skates are pointing.

**2** He is using vertical weight transfers (knee bends) to put pressure on his skate blades, which helps him execute the two-foot stop.

**3** Giroux's feet are staggered slightly. This helps him stabilize himself, but it also indicates he is likely using this two-foot stop in a drive and delay, which separates him from his defender.

**4** Reacting to Giroux's delay, the defender is executing a backward-to-forward transition to maintain a close gap. He uses the inside edges of both of his skates to stop his backward movement and transition quickly to forward movement (see page 78).

# Forward Power Start

Accelerating quickly from a stop or off a forward glide can give you a huge advantage when racing to loose pucks and breaking away from checkers. A lot of hockey happens in "small area" game situations, such as moving from a standstill to race to a loose puck off a face-off; quickness in areas like these can be even more important than overall speed.

## V-Start

There are two types of starts: the V-start (or heels-in start) and the cross-over start.

For the V-start, line up square to your desired direction of travel, with your heels in and together and your toes pointing out. You should have a deep knee bend (lower than you would for normal forward striding) with a forward lean, and your heels should be underneath you so you can use your body weight to help maximize the pressure on your blades. Start by driving off the inside edge of one skate with a thrust from the ball of your foot.

## Cross-Over Start

For a cross-over start, begin with your feet parallel and your skates and body at 90 degrees to your desired direction of travel. Again, a knee bend deeper than a standard striding knee bend is needed, and your weight should be evenly distributed along your blades. Lead with your back foot and begin with one cross-over—thrust from the

### Cross-Over Start

**1** Shea Weber's shoulders are square to his direction of travel, and his arms are in the hockey-playing position, holding the stick properly to handle the puck.

**2** Weber has nearly completed his initial drive with his left foot by crossing his skate under his right foot. His drive comes from the outside edge of his blade at the ball of his foot.

**3** Weber's right foot is positioned to strike the ice with a flat blade. He will continue his power start by driving off the inside edge at the ball of this foot, rotating it 90 degrees to his direction of travel to maximize his thrust.

ball of your foot. Follow immediately with a front foot cross-under as your back foot crosses over, pushing from the pad of your foot on the outside edge of your cross-under skate. As you move through the cross-over and cross-under, rotate your upper body until you are square to your desired direction of travel and ready to stride forward.

## Techniques After the Start

With both methods, there are three different techniques you can use to get going:

1 Immediately take a full stride;

2 run on the balls of your feet for three steps and then take a full stride;

3 run on the balls of your feet for two to three quick steps and then start striding, beginning with short strides and increasing to full strides.

Some players have great success with an immediate full stride, provided they are able to quickly and fully recover; this works well for some smaller or lighter players. Other players have greater success with three running steps before taking a full stride. The ideal method for most players is the third technique, as it combines a quick running start with shorter initial strides to ensure the drive leg recovers quickly. However, you should try all three techniques and both methods to see which suits you best.

**FIG. 26 V-Start**

**Drive foot rotates out toward a 90 degree angle as you push evenly off the inside edge of the ball of the drive foot. Keep your other foot close to the ice as you prepare to get in position for your next explosive drive.**

**FIG. 27**

**Cross-Over Start**

**As you cross-over with your back foot, your shoulders will rotate to become square to your direction of travel. Keep the blade of your stick toward the center of your body. Note that the toe of the cross-over skate is rotated slightly outward. When it lands it will immediately be ready to drive off the inside edge of the ball of the foot. Your front foot will complete a cross-under before your first stride.**

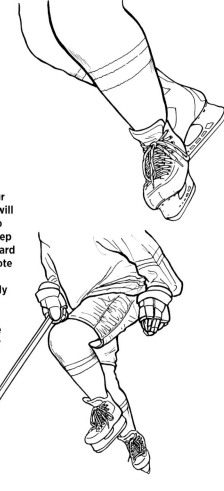

## Notes

It is crucial that you make the driving steps from the inside edge of your blades at the balls of your feet, not your toes. This ensures that your toes are rotated out as far as possible, making your skates close to 90 degrees to your line of travel and giving you more blade and a better angle to push off of. When running or using short strides, do not extend you ankles, as this delays the recovery of your drive foot. Move your arms forward in your direction of travel. While running or doing short strides, moving your arms in the proper skating motion will help you accelerate.

Quickly recovering your feet is a key ingredient to a quick start. You must move your feet as quickly as possible to ensure an explosive start.

# Backward Power Start

⬤ Getting a fast, straight backward start can be the difference between stopping a play or allowing an odd player rush or, even worse, a breakaway. It can also help you quickly get open for a shot or a pass.

### From Start to Cross-Over

To power start backward, rotate your lower body so that your skates are parallel and 90 degrees to your intended direction. Transfer your weight to your front skate—this will become your drive skate. With a deep knee bend, push off your drive skate and extend your leg in front of you. With pressure on your inside edge, rock from the heel to the ball of your foot and extend your ankle away from you and down into the ice; thrust straight backward off your inside edge at the ball of your foot.

After you thrust straight backward, lift your drive skate off the ice and cross it over your glide skate, which will have pivoted underneath you so that your heel is pointing in your intended direction of travel and you are gliding straight backward.

### Cross-Under and Stride

As soon as your drive skate lands from your cross-over, execute a cross-under with your glide skate. Push straight back with the outside edge of your skate at the pad of your foot and extend

**FIG. 28 Start Position**

**Weight is transferred to your front foot, resulting in a deep knee bend. Drive backward off the inside edge of your entire blade, rocking from the heel of your foot to the ball of your foot for extra thrust.**

# Backward Power Start Cross-Over to Cross-Under

**①** Brooks Orpik's shoulders and torso are square, opposite to his direction of travel.

**②** Orpik has pushed off his right leg (the original drive leg) and has nearly finished the cross-over portion of the backward power start. When his right leg touches the ice, this skate will glide while the left skate crosses under and thrusts back.

**③** Orpik is completing the cross-under with his left foot, with a thrust from the outside edge, at the ball of his foot. Orpik will conclude the cross-under by rotating his ankle to get as much of his outside edge on the ice as possible. Once this foot recovers, he will stride with his right foot.

your leg behind the heel of your cross-over skate. As your leg is fully extended, push your ankle down toward the ice to thrust off the outside edge of your blade at the pad of your foot. During your cross-under, glide backward on your cross-over skate.

Quickly recover your cross-under skate to a position underneath your body and beside your glide skate, and tap the insides of your skates together. Stride backward with the entire blade of your original drive skate, extending your leg fully out in front of you. Extend your ankle

and thrust into the ice off the inside edge of this skate at the ball of your foot. Continue alternating drive legs as you stride backward.

## Notes

Crossing over, then crossing under and then striding backward is important because this chain of movement will keep you on as straight a line as possible.

To help you complete the transition and correctly position your skates, you can think, "over, under, stride" in relation to your movements and "inside, outside, inside" in relation to the edge-work of your skates. It is also important to touch your skates together under you after you complete the cross-under, as this will ensure that your first backward stride is a full one.

**FIG. 29**

## Leg Extension from the Drive

Leg is extended so that you drive straight back. The ankle is extended down and away from you, driving the inside edge of your blade at the ball of your foot into the ice.

**FIG. 30 Cross-Over**

Recover your drive skate in toward your body and cross it over your gliding skate, which will have pivoted so that your heel is pointing toward your intended direction of travel.

**FIG. 31 Cross-Under**

Your original drive skate is the glide skate during your cross-under. Extend your cross-under leg behind the heel of your glide skate. Rotate and extend your ankle on your cross-under skate to drive from the outside edge at the pad of your foot. Recover this skate underneath your body and beside your glide skate, and tap the insides of your skates together before striding with your original drive skate.

# Rolling Your Wrists

Rolling your wrists is *the* fundamental puckhandling movement. When rolling your wrists you create a cradling or cupping effect with the blade of your stick that allows you to control the puck. You must be able to roll your wrists in order to increase the control and range of movement that is available to you when handling the puck away from your body—it will also help you perform more advanced puckhandling skills. It is essential that you become adept at rolling your wrists with your hands and arms in various positions in order to master advanced puckhandling moves.

## Cradling a Rolling Puck

**1** Brent Burns is holding his stick with the proper top-hand grip, and he has rolled his wrist to cup the puck on forehand.

**2** His bottom hand is loosely holding his stick, allowing the shaft to rotate and move up and down through his bottom hand as needed. He is rolling his wrist in order to help him handle the puck in close to his body and cup it.

## Practice

In order to cup the blade around or toward the puck, you must rotate your top hand by rolling your wrist. Here is the best way to learn how to roll your wrists:

**1** While in the hockey-playing position with a puck in front of you and in the middle of your body and with both hands on your stick, place the heel of your stick on the puck.

**2** Rotate your top hand so the toe of the stick touches the ice on one side and then on the other side of the puck. On your first attempt keep your bottom-hand grip loose so you can feel the shaft of the stick turn in your palm. On your second pass, grip with your bottom hand more tightly so that it too is rotating with the top hand. Repetition of this rotation is called rolling your wrists.

**3** Try rotating with your top hand only and then with your bottom hand only. Use a proper grip and rotate your hands so that the palm of each hand is facing up and then down.

## Method

To puckhandle, stand in the hockey-playing position with a puck in front of you and in the middle of your body and roll your wrists. Start with the stick on the ice beside the puck and lift the stick ever so slightly over the puck as you alternately cup the puck with the front of the blade and then cup the puck with the back of the blade. When you are not lifting the stick over the puck, there should be as much contact as possible between the blade and the puck. Handle the puck in the middle of the blade. As you progress, practice handling the puck toward the heel and the toe of the blade, always keeping the blade square to the ice.

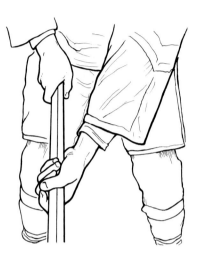

**FIG. 33 Backhand**
Proper hand and wrist position to cup the puck on the backhand while in the hockey-playing position.

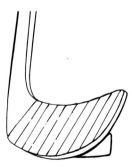 

**FIG. 32 Blade Rotation**
Proper blade rotation for cupping the puck on the backhand and forehand while executing basic puckhandling.

**FIG. 34 Forehand**
Proper hand and wrist position to cup the puck on the forehand while in the hockey-playing position.

# Extending Your Reach

 Handling the puck away from your body, either to the forehand side or to the backhand side, is a vital tool that will help you protect the puck and allow you to change the angle of your attacks and shots.

## Forehand Drive with Extension

**1** Connor McDavid drives around his opponent by combining a cross-under with a forehand extension. McDavid has moved his bottom hand up the shaft of his stick to extend his reach. He could further protect the puck by releasing his top hand from his stick and using it to fend off the defensive player. To do this, McDavid would need to roll the wrist of his bottom hand to have it face palm down. This will create a cradle as he carries the puck.

**2** McDavid's cross-over foot is about to hit the ice. When it does, he will continue his deep knee bend and move his hands and chest down, closer to the ice, and over his knee. This will enable him to further extend his reach and cradle the puck to protect it from the defender.

**3** When McDavid's cross-under leg recovers, it will come between him and the defender, adding another layer of puck protection to his drive.

### Notes

When extending your reach as explained in Fig. 35, it is important to push your top hand under the forearm of your bottom hand so that the blade of your stick is square to the ice and the toe is pointed ahead. When most players are at maximum extension, their bottom hand will be close to one fist-length from their top hand. This will allow you to pass or shoot when your reach is extended to your forehand side. Some elite players are able to extend their reach to the point that their bottom hand will touch their

**FIG. 35 Forehand Extension**

Bring your top hand underneath the forearm of your bottom hand and slide your bottom hand up, toward your top hand. Roll your wrists to cup the puck, and extend further by bending your same-side knee.

**FIG. 36 Backhand Extension**

Move your top hand out and away from your body on your backhand side. Slide your bottom hand up, toward your top hand. Roll your wrists to cup the puck, and extend further by bending your off-side knee.

top hand. On the backhand it is common for your hands to touch when at maximum extension. Releasing a shot from this position with any strength is an elite-level skill.

To increase your extension, to either your backhand side or your forehand side, you can "break" your wrists, which is extreme wrist rolling. You break your wrists so that your stick blade angles away from you as far as it can. To further increase your extension, you can lower your hands and bend the knee closest to the puck. Putting your hands and body closer to the ice enables you to extend further then you would be able to from an upright position.

**Extra Extension**
Johnny Gaudreau extends his reach to collect a loose puck. He adds extra reach by lowering his hands and chest over the knee closest to the puck.

# Traditional Pass: Forehand or Backhand

Hockey is a team game. It is also a game of puck possession. In order to keep possession of the puck, players need to be able to pass it accurately. The very best players are great passers and pass receivers who are able to make all the players around them better.

## Short Forehand Pass

**1** Corey Perry keeps his head up as he looks at his target. He is sweeping the puck, which started "back of center," forward to the release point. As he moves the puck across his body, he moves his top and bottom hands away from his body and drops the shoulder of his bottom arm.

**2** Perry's legs and feet are nearly perpendicular to his target as he sweeps the puck from back of the center of his body (near his same foot) and releases it ahead of the center of his body (toward his off foot).

**3** Perry keeps his blade square to his target as he follows through. He opens his blade up and can execute a flat pass or a saucer pass.

### Method

Stand in the hockey-skating position with your skates 90 degrees to your target. Roll your wrists to put the puck in the middle of the blade, keep your head up and look at your target. You should be in the same position you are in when puckhandling while moving forward, with your top hand out from your body. To initiate the passing motion, bring the puck back of "center" (an imaginary line drawn on the ice running up between your skates)—this motion will bring your top hand across your body to your same side during a forehand pass and across your body to your off side during a backhand pass. From this position, with the puck cradled and back of center, sweep the puck toward your target with the blade of your stick square to the target. Release the puck from the center of the blade and follow through with your stick. For a long pass, roll your wrists over and follow through by pointing the blade of your stick at your target; for a short pass, follow through by moving both your top and bottom hands away from your body, keeping the blade square to your target. In both forehand and backhand passes, the top hand travels across your body.

## Tip

Practice making passes when stationary and with your feet 90 degrees to your target (duplicating two players skating forward in the same direction) as well as with your feet facing your target. Practice making passes both off two feet and off one foot and, in particular, off your same foot (i.e. left foot for left-handed players and right foot for right-handed players). Practice these passes while in motion, too.

You can also work on quick-release passes—receiving and making a pass in one motion. Remember to always try to sweep

**Backhand Pass**
Devin Shore looks to make a backhand pass. The puck is slightly back of center, and Shore rotates his stick to cup the puck and sweep it forward. Like in a forehand pass, his shoulders and torso rotate while his feet stay 90 degrees to his target. Most importantly, Shore's top hand stays out from his body for strength and accuracy.

**FIG. 37**
**Short Pass Final Position**
**When passing to a teammate close to you, use a short follow-through: move both your top and bottom hands away from your body and keep your blade square to your target.**

the puck. Even with quick-release passes, the pass should be received by rolling your wrists and cupping the puck, and then it should be quickly swept toward the target,

not snapped. It is also important to keep your top hand away from your body to ensure your passes are controlled and accurate. This is particularly true with backhand passes, as many players tend to have their top hand too close to their body on a backhand pass, resulting in weak and inaccurate passes. The sweeping motion and follow-through of a backhand pass will take your top hand across your body.

# Same-Foot Pass

Passing from your same foot is a great way to deliver a quick-release pass or a pass while skating. The motion used is nearly identical to that of a same-foot shot, which means you can also use it to make a pass off of a fake shot.

Unlike a traditional pass, in which you sweep the puck from your back foot to your front foot, for a same-foot pass you sweep the puck from near your heel to ahead of your toe on your forehand side. You thereby force your body to be square to the direction the pass is meant to travel; both your toes and your shoulders will be facing your intended target. In a traditional pass, your toes are pointing 90 degrees to your target.

Players often use same-foot passes when they want to pass while skating forward, since the pass is made during the forward stride, when the same-side foot is gliding and the off-side foot is striding. This keeps your body square to your direction of travel and to the pass, and it allows you to move up with the play. It is a great pass to make when you want to skate ahead of the pass receiver for a give-and-go opportunity.

## Same-Foot Snap Pass

**1** Brandon Manning eyes Jakub Voracek in the high slot. His head is up and his shoulders are square to his target.

**2** Manning has the puck on his same side, in line with the heel of his same foot. He is rolling his wrists to cup the puck on contact. As he sweeps the puck from his heel to a release point ahead of him, he will do so with a snapping motion (similar to executing a snap shot; see page 66).

**3** Manning is holding his hands close to his body but out from his hips to give him room to move through the passing motion.

## Method

With your body square to your target, both of your skates facing straight ahead and your head up, bring the puck beside the heel of your same foot. Keep your stick blade square and your hands close to your body. As you move the puck to your same side, you'll naturally shift your weight to your same foot. This will apply pressure to your stick, which you can use for your pass. (When shooting, you'll want to move all of your weight onto your same foot to help load energy into your shot. For a pass, you can move less weight and apply less pressure to your stick.) Sweep the puck forward with a firm grip and follow-through. For a long pass you'll want to roll your wrists as you would for a wrist shot (see page 62). For a shorter pass you'll want to keep your stick blade square to your target by moving your hands away from your body (see Fig. 37 on page 53).

# Saucer Pass

Sometimes you will need to pass the puck over an opposing player's stick or even their leg or body. In this instance you will want the puck to go up off the ice, over the obstacle and then return to the ice flat so the receiving player can handle the pass. The best way to do this is to use a saucer pass. This type of pass gets its name from the fact that the puck travels in the air like a saucer or Frisbee. It stays flat while it rotates through the air and when it lands on the ice.

## Mid-release of Wrist Saucer Pass

**1** Auston Matthews is in the midst of moving the puck from the heel of his stick to its toe in order to execute a saucer pass. To do this, he is rapidly moving his hands from his left to his right, effectively cutting his blade across the puck.

**2** He is rolling his wrists to open the blade of his stick, to help elevate the puck. This, along with the cutting action he is preforming with the stick blade, has already started to lift the puck from the ice. He is keeping his hands away from his body so he is free to move them quickly in order to add rotation when he releases the puck.

**FIG. 38 Start: Heel**
**Start your wrist saucer pass with the puck slightly ahead of you on your stick side. Keep your hands away from your body and to your forehand side. The puck is at the heel of your stick. Keep your blade open and your knees bent.**

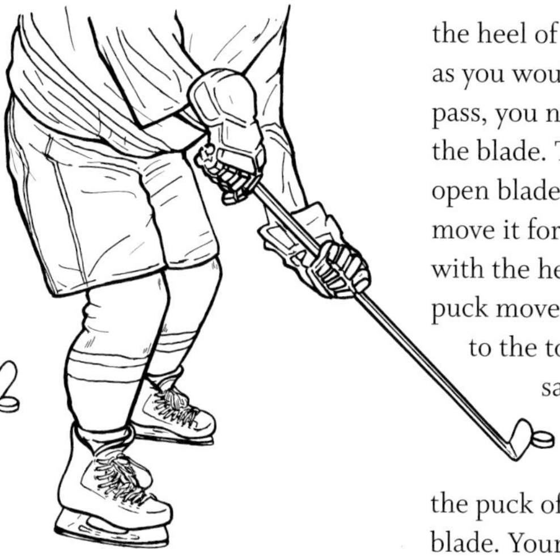

## Wrist Saucer

The "wrist" saucer pass is the easiest version of the saucer pass. Start by opening the blade of your stick (a closed blade is one that cups the puck) with the puck on the heel of the angled blade. Initiate the pass with both of your hands away from your body and with your shoulders square to your target. Quickly move your hands across your body toward your backhand side. This movement will simultaneously move your hands in toward your body as it sends the puck from the heel of the blade to the toe, where it is released—you are cutting your blade across the puck. The harder and quicker you do this (along with how open the blade is), the higher, faster and flatter your pass will be.

**FIG. 39 Finish: Toe**
**Quickly bring your hands in toward your body and move them across your body toward your off side. This will roll the puck, from the heel to the toe, along your open stick blade. As the puck reaches the toe, raise your stick off the ice as you follow through to your off side. If your blade is open and you move your hands very quickly, this will spin the puck and send it airborne.**

The puck will spin counterclockwise for a left-handed player and clockwise for a right-handed player as it travels through the air.

## Snap Saucer

The closer the receiving player is to you, the more difficult it is for you to make a good saucer pass. For very short passes, a "snap" saucer pass is more efficient: it gets the puck in the air quickly with a quicker release. This technique is often used when the puck is in a passing position away from your body.

The technique for the snap saucer pass is the same as for the wrist saucer pass, except that instead of rolling the puck from the heel of the blade to the toe, as you would for the wrist saucer pass, you need to snap the puck off the blade. To do this, bring your open blade back and then quickly move it forward to strike the puck with the heel of the blade. The puck movement from the heel to the toe of the blade is the same, but you should move more quickly.

The velocity will snap the puck off the toe of the open blade. Your hand movement is still across and toward your body, but your hands do not have to travel as far, allowing you to release the puck more quickly. It takes much more practice to be accurate with a snap saucer pass than with a wrist saucer pass. Many players use a snap saucer pass when executing a backhand saucer pass.

## Tip

To practice spinning the puck, pass with a teammate using the technique outlined above but keep the puck on the ice. Try to see how quickly you can move your hands in order to make the puck spin as quickly as possible. Once you are able to spin the puck and slide it on the ice to your target, then you can start to grip the puck more with the heel of the blade and follow through higher with the blade after you release the puck in order to start to lift it off the ice while it rotates. Eventually you will be able to lift the puck right off the ice and perform a perfect saucer pass.

# Receiving a Pass

 The key to controlling your reception of a pass is to reverse the motion you make when releasing a pass.

## Method

Receiving a puck to your stick is a lot like catching a football: you must absorb the energy from the object. In order to do this, move your stick away from your body and extend your arms slightly toward your target as you bring the blade out to "meet" the puck (especially for pucks that are passed with a lot of force). It is crucial that you keep your stick on the ice with the blade square to the ice, which provides a target for the passer. Upon receiving the puck, "catch" the pass by rolling your wrists so that the blade moves back and cups the puck. This absorbs the energy of the pass and helps you control the puck. Keeping your top hand away from your body and rotating your top hand to cup the blade are keys to successfully receiving passes.

**FIG. 40 Reception Positions**
The principles used to receive a pass apply to both the forehand and the backhand. Your blade should be cupped when catching a pass, as it will help you control the puck by absorbing the energy of the pass.

## Receiving a Pass in Motion

**1** Connor Carrick's hands are out from his body as he brings his stick out to meet a hard pass.

**2** Carrick's stick blade is square to the ice in anticipation of the pass. When he receives the pass, he will rotate his top hand to cup his blade and "catch" the pass. He will move his arms and the blade of his stick in toward his body and to his off side to help absorb the energy of the pass.

# Receiving Off-Target Passes

● The key to controlling your reception of an off-target pass is to keep your stick blade square to the ice, as opposed to having only the heel or the toe of the blade receive the pass.

## Receiving in Feet

**1** P.K. Subban's shoulders are square to the incoming puck. He is raising his top-hand and arm and pushing them from his body so he can place his stick blade between his feet, which are spread wide. His wrist is rolled to rotate the blade of his stick, which cups his blade so he can catch the pass.

**2** Subban's bottom hand is low on the shaft of his stick to keep the blade square to the ice. He is pinching his right elbow in by his chest as he rolls his wrist to cup his stick blade and catch the puck.

### Receiving Off-Target Passes on the Forehand

To receive a pass anywhere between the heel of your stick and your off skate, or even outside your off skate, move your stick blade to the puck by keeping your top hand up and away from your body. Slide your bottom hand low on the shaft of your stick while you lower your body. This ensures your blade is flat and square to the puck. The closer the puck is to your off foot, the further your bottom hand must move down the shaft of your stick and the further your top hand will be pushed to your off side.

Elite players will lower their body, sometimes to the point of putting a knee on the ice, to shoot the puck after receiving the pass. This technique is great for shooting pucks off of passes that are well in on your feet.

If the pass is coming so quickly at your feet that you don't have time to get the stick blade into position, use your skate blade to receive the pass and deflect the puck to your stick or to where you can reach the puck and bring it under control. Angle your skate blade to deflect the puck to where you want it to go.

When the pass is ahead of the blade, accept the pass by extending and moving the stick blade forward, keeping it square to the puck. To do this, extend your top hand away from your body and move your bottom hand progressively up the shaft until, at the furthest point, it touches your top hand. To reach even further, release your bottom hand from the stick, extending and allowing your top hand to move the stick further ahead so the blade can receive the pass.

### Receiving Off-Target Passes on the Backhand

If you are receiving an off-target pass on your off side on the backhand side of your blade, whether in your feet or ahead of you, you use the same hand movements as when receiving an off-target pass on your forehand. If the pass is between the heel of your stick and

**Moving into an Off-Target Pass**

Keith Yandle moves his top hand out and his bottom hand low on his stick shaft to bring his stick blade square to the ice in anticipation of recieving an off-target pass. He has picked up his same foot in anticipation of immediately moving into the path of the pass upon reception. He will drive his body in this new direction with his off foot.

**FIG. 41**

### Passes Ahead of You

Keep both feet planted on the ice and extend your reach by moving your top hand as far across your body as you can. At the same time bring your bottom hand up toward your top hand. Keep your arm raised to keep your blade square to the ice.

your off skate, move your bottom hand down the shaft of your stick and move your top hand across your body and out from your body toward your off side.

If the pass is ahead of your stick blade, extend your reach as illustrated on page 50.

If you are receiving the pass between the heel of your stick and your feet on the backhand side of your blade toward your same side, bring your top hand across your body toward the forearm of your bottom hand. The closer the puck is to your feet, the further your top hand will move across your body and underneath the forearm of your bottom hand.

# Wrist Shot

This is the shot most players will learn first. It can be very accurate, especially if you keep your head up through the shooting motion.

## Technique

The technique of a traditional wrist shot is similar to the technique of a forehand pass. When executing a basic wrist shot, stand 90 degrees to your target with your skates parallel. Bring the puck back of center (an imaginary line drawn on the ice running up between your skates), and then sweep the puck forward while you transfer your weight from your back skate (the skate furthest from the target) to your front skate (the skate closest to the target).

## All in the Wrists

With the puck back of center, roll your wrists to close your blade over the puck and "grip" the puck toward the heel of the blade. As you sweep the puck forward, roll your wrists to open the blade up, allowing the puck to travel up the blade. Upon release, roll your wrists a third time, closing the blade over the puck and whipping it off the middle of the blade toward the toe. The entire motion is: blade closed, open, closed.

## Weight and Follow-Through

As you pull the puck back, move your hands back and in slightly toward your body, and keep your weight on your back foot with your back leg bent. Quickly sweep the puck forward as close to your body as comfortably possible, and quickly transfer your weight to your front skate, bending your front leg. Release the shot from the center of your body, and move your blade quickly forward. Follow through on the shot by extending your bottom hand toward your target and point your stick at it.

To get extra velocity on the shot, press your bottom hand down on the shaft of the stick (which will cause the stick to flex) just before you release. This flexing will create a whip in the stick that will add a "kick" to the puck upon release.

## Tips

* Quick hand speed and wrist rolling are very important for a quick release and a fast shot. As in all shots, stick speed is crucial to the speed of your shot.
* Your bottom hand should be lower down the shaft of the stick than when stick-handling.
* Keeping your hands close to your body as they pass across your body makes it easier to add power to the shot through pressure on the stick.

## Wrist Shot

**1** Mike Green's top hand is very close to his body. He rolls his wrist, closing the blade as he grips the puck.

**2** Green's bottom hand is a little less than halfway down the shaft of his stick. His bottom hand is beginning to load pressure on the shaft, which will increase as he straightens his bottom arm and applies more pressure throughout the shooting motion.

**3** Green's right foot lifts from the ice as a result of the torque created by the power and weight that is transferred from his back foot (right foot) to his front foot (left foot).

**4** Green's stick flexes from the pressure he applied with his bottom hand at the beginning of the sequence.

**5** Green whips the puck off the blade of his stick, between the middle and toe. As the puck leaves his stick, Green will roll his wrists again to close the blade during his follow-through.

✳ The speed of your follow-through will add power to your shot. Extending your bottom hand through the follow-through will allow you to use your core and your back to add power to your shot.

✳ The follow-through can determine the height of your shot. A high follow-through and an open blade on the follow-through will send the puck higher, while a low follow-through and closed blade will send the puck lower.

✳ If possible, keep your head up throughout the shooting motion, so that you can keep your eye on your target and adjust accordingly.

### Advanced

Elite players disguise their release of the puck by shooting while puckhandling, often off of their same foot.

Elite players also learn to change the position of the puck just before releasing it, thus changing the angle of the shot. To do this, either draw the puck in closer to your body before shooting or extend your arms and push the puck away from your body before shooting. For the latter, extend your arms away from your body and move your bottom hand closer to your top hand. You lose a lot of power on this shot, but changing the position of the puck and the angle of the shot can create scoring opportunities. This technique is great when used close to the goal after a deke. The key is to shoot the puck as quickly as possible after you have changed the angle.

# Backhand Shot

The principles that apply to the wrist shot also apply to the backhand shot, except that the backhand shot almost always involves a transfer of weight from the off foot (i.e., back) to the same foot (i.e., front). It is extremely hard to get any power on a backhand shot unless you transfer your weight. Many players can shoot off two feet with their weight evenly distributed or off their off foot with their arms extended, but these techniques are used almost exclusively close to the goal, particularly after a deke or quick move to the backhand.

## Gripping the Puck on the Backhand

**1** Brad Richardson's top hand is out from his body, allowing it to move freely across his chest when he sweeps the puck forward. His wrist is rolled to close his blade over the puck.

**2** He drops his left shoulder and keeps his head down after he pulls the puck back. Richardson pulls his stick through the shooting motion with his bottom hand, applying pressure and flexing his stick.

**3** He transfers his weight from his back (off) foot to his front (same) foot as he sweeps the puck forward.

### Method

To execute a basic backhand shot, stand 90 degrees to your target with your skates parallel. As with the traditional wrist shot, bring the puck back of center and roll your wrists to cup the puck. Cup the back of the blade over the puck, with the puck at the heel of your blade. Sweep the puck forward and roll your wrists to open the blade, allowing the puck to move up the blade from the heel, and then close the blade again before you release the puck. Throughout the movement, transfer your weight from your off foot to your same foot. (The shoulder on your same side will drop a little as you bend your same-side knee to transfer your weight and drive the puck forward.) Concentrate on cradling the puck blade between the heel and center of the closed blade, and release the puck off the middle of your blade. Follow through with a closed blade, drive your bottom hand toward your target and point the blade at your target.

Apply pressure on the shaft of the stick during the release to flex the stick and help whip the puck. Remember to drive the puck using your arms, shoulders and back, not just your wrists. The more open your blade and the higher your follow-through, the higher the puck will go. In order to keep the puck low, keep your blade closed and your follow-through low.

## Common Problems

A major mistake made by many players when shooting a backhand is to open the blade on the release in order to flip or lift the puck. This is a good technique to use when you are close to the net but not when shooting from out far. Another common error is to keep the top hand too close to the body when starting the shot. Make sure your top hand is up and away from your body so you can sweep it across your body and maximize the power of your shot.

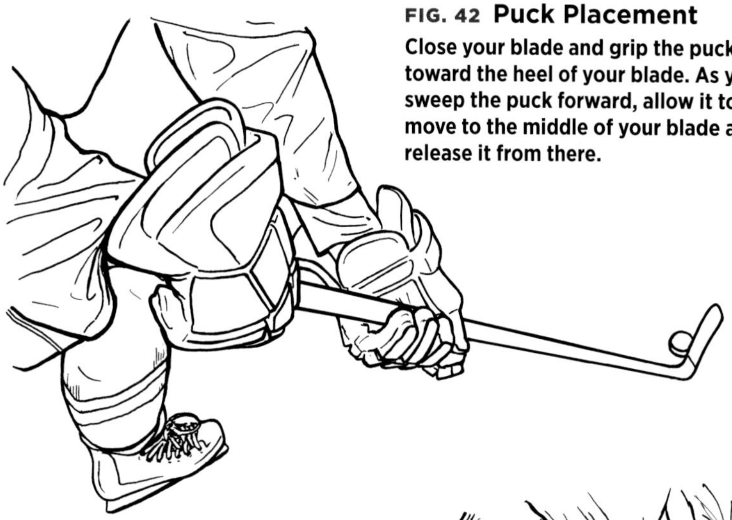

**FIG. 42 Puck Placement**
Close your blade and grip the puck toward the heel of your blade. As you sweep the puck forward, allow it to move to the middle of your blade and release it from there.

## Backhand Advantages

✳ **Concealment:** When the puck is brought back on the backhand, prior to being released, it can be concealed by the body, which makes it difficult for a goalie to pick up its location. This is particularly true if the drive leg (the front leg) is well bent just before shooting.

✳ **Deception:** With little indication (other than the angle of the blade) as to where a backhand shot is going, goalies often think that a backhand shot will be high. As a result, if you rotate your hands and close the blade over the puck on the follow-through and shoot the puck low with a low follow-through, it will often surprise a goalkeeper, as the puck will stay closer to the ice.

✳ **Top-shelf shooting:** When close to the net, it is more natural to shoot the puck with an open blade from the backhand side

**FIG. 43 Release**
Upon release, rotate your stick so the blade is closed and point it at your target. A low release will give you a low shot, a high release a high shot. Transfer all of your weight onto your front (same) foot to give the shot as much power as possible.

than it is from the forehand side, making it easier to get the puck up quickly without having to change the position of your body. Deke to the backhand and shoot the puck high!

# Snap Shot

A snap shot is your quick-release shot. It is the first shot you'll learn where the blade is not in constant contact with the puck throughout the shooting motion. You don't bring the blade as far back from the puck as you do for a slap shot. Instead, the blade is only brought back a short distance, and sometimes the blade doesn't even leave the ice. A snapshot can be very effective for one-timers from your off wing, off your off foot, or when combined with a toe drag and a change of the angle of the puck.

## Technique

The snap shot can be taken from anywhere on your forehand side and can be released traditionally (by moving your weight from back to front, as in the pictures here), off of your same foot or off of both feet. Once you bring your blade back and away from the puck, immediately explode forward onto the puck, striking it with the middle of your blade and sending it quickly forward.

## All in the Wrists

Upon contact, the blade of your stick should be square to the ice; your blade can actually strike the ice just before the puck. When striking the puck, roll your wrists quickly to close your blade then open your blade then go back to a closed blade—the same motion as in a wrist shot. You must roll your wrists extremely quickly as the movement coincides with the blade "moving through" the puck. This is often referred to as "snapping" the puck. Your bottom hand should be slightly lower down on the shaft of the stick than when taking a wrist shot. Grip the stick very tightly with both hands during the shooting motion.

## Follow-Through

You can make a snap shot with very little follow-through, relying on a quick stick to explode onto the puck and add speed through the shot, or you can use a strong follow-through similar to the follow-through of a slap shot. When you combine a toe drag movement with a snap shot, you can use a strong follow-through, similar to a wrist shot, to provide speed and accuracy to your shot. The height of your follow-through determines the height of your shot.

## Combination Wrist Shot–Snap Shot

You can use this shot to change the position of the puck prior to your shot. It also disguises the snap shot. The set up for this shot is the same as for a traditional wrist shot, but you use a snap-shot release.

First change the position of the

## Snap Shot Set-Up to Release

**1** The puck is well back of center and Artemi Panarin's stick blade is square on the ice and separated from the puck, giving Panarin space to explode onto the puck.

**2** He is rolling his top wrist to close the blade of his stick. He will roll his wrists and open his blade slightly as he explodes onto the puck. His blade will open throughout the course of the shot and close — the snap — as the puck leaves his stick.

**3** Panarin strikes the puck with the middle of his blade. As he finishes the shot, the puck will move slightly toward the toe of his blade, but by snapping his wrists to close the blade he will keep the puck on its intended trajectory. If he doesn't roll his wrists quickly for the snap, the puck will fly off the toe off the stick and toward the direction of the camera.

**4** Panarin's same knee dips as he rotates his shoulders through the shot and applies pressure to the shaft of his stick with his bottom hand. This pressure flexes the stick, providing whip that adds speed to his shot.

puck by pulling it toward your body. Bring the middle and heel of the blade up and back from the puck while keeping the toe of the stick on the ice. To release the puck, drive the middle and heel of the blade forward and snap the puck. This shot can be made from the off or same foot. Mark Messier shot the puck very effectively on his off wing using this technique.

### FIG. 44 Explosive Release

The key to a snap shot is to quickly explode your stick onto the puck, as you can move your stick faster without the puck than with it. You can still do this while having some contact with the puck: cradle (or drag) the puck with the toe of your stick and then explode onto the puck with the heel of your stick. Release the puck from the middle of the blade.

# Slap Shot

A slap shot can be devastatingly hard and fast, but it can also take a while to release and is often a shooter's least accurate shot. However, if you can harness the strength of the slap shot, it can be deadly.

## Method

To start, position yourself with your feet 90 degrees to your target and place the puck in the middle of your body but slightly toward your front foot. The backswing of a slap shot can vary from a shorter "half" backswing, which stays parallel to the ice, to a full backswing, in which the stick is raised much higher and is almost vertical. During the backswing, rotate your hands as you would when drawing the blade back just before releasing a snap shot, and place your bottom hand slightly lower down on the shaft of the stick than when taking a snap shot. Ensure the blade is closed over the puck when it makes contact with it, and snap your wrists when you release. Strike the puck with the middle of the blade and ensure the blade is square to the ice. Your stick should strike the ice just behind the puck. Be sure to keep the puck close enough to your body so that you can place full pressure on the shaft of the stick with your bottom hand. This pressure will flex and whip the stick, which will help propel the puck.

## Follow-Through

The entire motion should be completed very quickly, as stick speed will affect the speed of your shot; make sure you transfer your weight from your back foot to your front foot quickly. A strong follow-through is also important and allows you to use your hips, back, shoulders and arms during the shot. You should follow through until your bottom hand is driven almost straight ahead, with the stick pointing at your target. As you drive your weight forward and follow through on the shot, your back leg may want to come up off the ice. This can add power to your shot by adding weight to the transfer that happens from back to front, and it also gives you more torque on the shot and a full extension of your arms on the follow-through. However, ending a slap shot on one foot requires great balance, as your body is moving forward and twisting with a great deal of power.

Try to keep your head up throughout the shooting motion. This will allow you to be more accurate; it will also enable you to change from a slap shot to a slap pass if the situation on the ice calls for it. Wayne Gretzky may have been the first player to use the "heads up" slap shot effectively.

## Slap Shot Set-Up to Release

**1** Brayden McNabb's head is up looking toward his target as he is about to strike the puck. His bottom hand is low on the shaft of his stick — lower than for any other shooting motion — creating flex as he transfers his weight from back to front, loading power on his stick.

**2** McNabb strikes with his blade flush to the ice before he makes contact with the puck, and he rotates his stick in a slightly closed position.

**3** McNabb drives his bottom hand forward through contact. The torque from the shot twists his body. He rotates his bottom hand, keeping his blade in a closed position through contact. He then snaps his wrists as he releases the shot, closing the blade as he follows through.

**4** The blade is pointing at the target — the higher the follow-through, the higher the shot.

**5** McNabb transfers his weight from his back leg to his front leg. He also lifts his back leg to apply more weight to the transfer (it is also lifted because of the amount of torque the shooting motion generated).

### Tip

The slap shot is very effective for one-time shots, particularly when you are on your off wing. A fake slap shot can also be very effective (see page 91). Players can drive off the fake and shoot while in motion or move the puck to a player who is in a better position to score a goal.

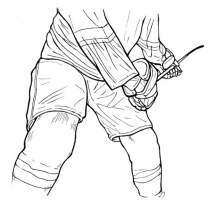

**FIG. 45 Backswing**
Your backswing can be small (low to the ice), medium (as illustrated here), or large (stick straight up in the air) depending on the amount of time you have. Regardless of your backswing type, be sure to load as much energy and weight onto your back foot as you can so that you can transfer that into your shot when you follow through to your front foot.

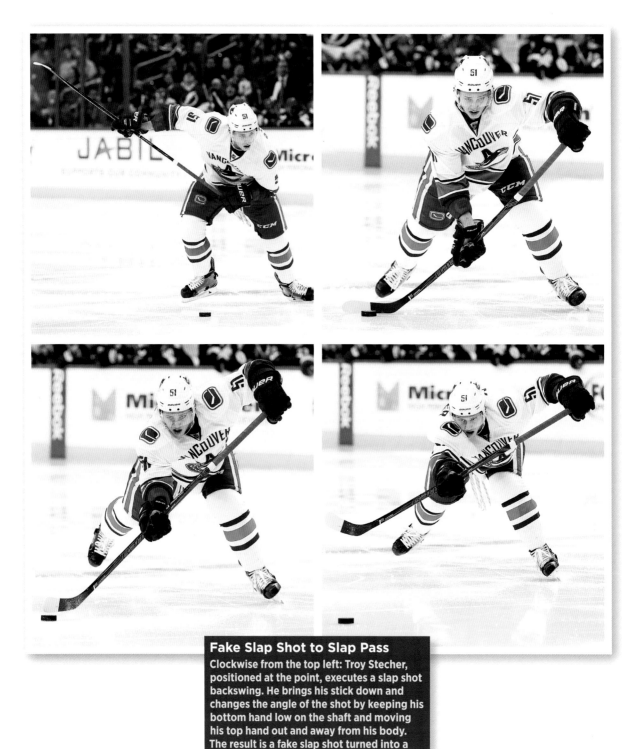

**Fake Slap Shot to Slap Pass**

Clockwise from the top left: Troy Stecher, positioned at the point, executes a slap shot backswing. He brings his stick down and changes the angle of the shot by keeping his bottom hand low on the shaft and moving his top hand out and away from his body. The result is a fake slap shot turned into a slap pass.

# Open-Bladed Shot

The best shot to use when close to a goalie who is covering the bottom part of the net is the open-bladed shot, as it enables a player to get the puck up and over the goalkeeper quickly. This shot can also be used when you need to get the puck up quickly, such as to clear the puck out of the defensive zone or dump it into the offensive zone.

## Shot in Tight to the Goal

1 Viktor Arvidsson's top and bottom hands are out and away from his body. He rotates his wrists to open up his blade and scoop the puck onto the middle of his blade.

2 Aiming for the open near-side corner of the net, he keeps his blade open throughout the shooting motion and follow-through, which he executes rapidly in order to get the puck up as high as possible as quickly as possible.

You can execute an open-bladed shot with a traditional release (standing 90 degrees to the target with your skates parallel) or by shooting off of your same foot or off both feet. You can use it on your forehand side or your backhand side. The key to a successful open-bladed shot is to rotate your hands so the blade is open while you are shooting. When the blade is open you can use a wrist-shot shooting motion to "wrist," or scoop, the puck up with the middle of your blade. You can also use a snap-shot motion, snapping the puck off the heel, middle or toe of the front of your blade. In either case, the shooting motion will start in closer to your body than with a regular wrist or snap shot. To help get the puck closer to your body, you need to move your top hand away from your body and your bottom hand down low on the shaft of your stick and bring your follow-through up high. This will enable you to shoot the puck up high very quickly. This shooting technique is very effective for scoring when close to the goalie.

# Same-Foot Shot

This is a deadly way to shoot, and a same-foot shot offers many advantages. You can use this technique many different ways, including: shooting in motion, shooting with a quick release on your proper side, shooting when moving laterally to your proper side and shooting with a deceptive release.

## Left-Handed Same-Foot Shot

**1** J.T. Miller's head is up and he's looking at his target; his shoulders are square to the target. His top hand is up high and in close to his shoulder, helping to create a slingshot-like whip from his stick.

**2** Miller's bottom hand is halfway down the shaft and is applying pressure to the shaft of his stick (through the heel of his hand) in order to flex the stick and create whip.

**3** Miller is transferring his body weight to his same foot by leaning to his same side and lifting his off foot from the ice (sometimes this will be in a kicking motion). This weight transfer applies extra pressure to the stick for extra kick on his shot. Miller's same-side foot is on a flat blade for balance and glide.

In simple terms, your "same" foot is the foot on the same side as the way you shoot—the right foot for right-handed players and the left foot for left-handed players. This is the foot to your "proper" or forehand side. The "off" foot is the foot opposite to the way you shoot—left foot for right-handed players and right foot for left-handed players. This is the foot to your "off" or backhand side.

When we refer to the foot that a player shoots off of in any given situation, we are referring to the foot that the player's weight is on when the shot is released. Many players will shoot from their "off" foot in certain circumstances, and in those circumstances that foot becomes the "front" foot (the foot closest to the target when the puck is released). The wrist shot is a great example of the off foot becoming the front foot. However, the same players will shoot from their "same" foot in other circumstances, when the same foot will become the "front" foot, as pictured to the left.

### Method

To shoot off your same foot, keep your body square to your target with both of your skates facing straight ahead and your head up. With your hands close to your body, bring the puck to your forehand side with your stick blade square to your target. When shooting, move all of your weight onto your same foot while applying pressure on your stick, forcing it to flex. Sweep the puck forward with a firm grip. Apply lots of pressure with your bottom hand, and roll your wrists the same as you would for a wrist shot. Follow through after the shot, driving your bottom hand forward and pointing your stick at your target.

## Tip

To gain more power on your shot, transfer more weight to your same foot by raising your off foot from the ice. Some players will "kick" their off foot by bending and then straightening their leg—kicking the air—as they put pressure on their stick.

## Same Foot Advantages

**＊ Deceptive puck release:** There are less physical indicators to tip off a goalie as to when to expect a shot (i.e., no weight transfer prior to the release), plus you can shoot in motion (i.e., dekes and drives to the net).

**＊ Quicker release from passes to your proper wing:** A lefty on the left wing or a righty on the right wing can collect

**Same-Foot Balance**
Tyler Seguin releases a same-foot shot in motion. He has moved all of his body weight onto his same foot and is balancing perfectly with his weight over a flat skate blade. Balance is a key component to a successful same-foot shot.

a pass and release it quicker because they don't have to rotate their body and shoot traditionally (transferring weight from the same foot to the off foot).

**＊ Deceptive off-wing shooting:** With shoulders square to the net, you can draw the puck in close to your body, changing the angle of the shot and concealing the timing of the release.

**＊ Accuracy:** You can keep your head up throughout the entire shooting motion.

**FIG. 46 Front View**
A front view of the same-foot shot. Note the body lean and the pressure applied on the middle of the shaft by the nearly straight bottom arm.

# 3 Next Level Skills

Joe Pavelski uses a knee-down shot to score against the Ottawa Senators. To read more on knee-down shots, see page 98.

# Forward-to-Backward Transition

If there is one thing that is constant in hockey, it is transition! You need to be able to move up the ice and back while always facing the play. There are numerous situations where a seamless transition from skating forward in one direction to skating backward in the opposite direction while staying square to the original direction of travel is needed, such as when the defense follows a play up the ice and there is a turnover or when a forward driving to the net gets in too deep and wants to move back into a better position while still facing the puck.

## Method One: Slide to Backward Power Start

Start a forward-to-backward transition by skating forward then making a forward lateral slide (see page 42). The lateral slide is then combined with a backward power start (see page 46). The slide ensures that some of your forward speed is maintained as you change direction, giving you momentum going into your power start. The backward power start (started while still in the slide motion) allows you to move backward quickly and efficiently.

When you reach the point of your lateral slide where you want to start going backward, bend the knee of your front leg and transfer your weight onto your front skate. As your weight comes off your back skate, pivot it so that the heel of your back skate is toward the direction you want to travel backward. Next, initiate a backward power start with your front skate: one cross-over, one cross-under, feet brought together and a backward stride. It is imperative that your thrust and ankle extension for both the power start and the cross-under are straight back and away from your direction of travel to keep you on as straight a line as possible.

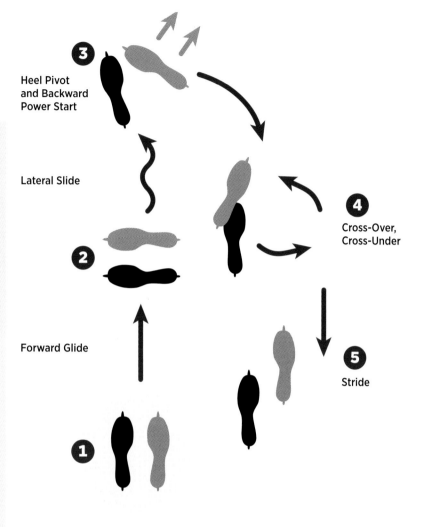

## Slide to Backward Power Start

**1** Patric Hornqvist is at the end of his lateral slide during his transition from skating forward to striding backward while continuously facing the play. Hornqvist's eyes are following the play. His heels point in the direction he initially intends to travel to accommodate the transition. The slide allows him to transfer forward momentum into backward speed.

**2** Hornqvist has begun to pick up his left foot in order to begin the cross-over, cross-under sequence of a backward power start (see page 46) that will propel him backward. His initial drive and cross-over will be with his left foot.

**FIG. 47 Method One: Slide to Backward Power Start**

## Method Two: The Pivot

If you are not advancing straight up the ice but are moving forward on an angle and don't need to maintain a straight line in your transition from forward to backward, you can use the forward-to-backward pivot to maintain speed through your transition.

As you are moving up the ice on an angle, glide forward with your skates shoulder width apart, parallel and facing forward. Next, raise your weight off your skates by straightening your legs, and pivot the heels of your skates so they point in your new direction of travel. At the same time, bend your knees to put pressure on the balls of your feet so you start skating backward in your new direction —the direction in which your heels are pointing. As you pivot and apply pressure you will glide backward, and from there you can choose to stride if needed. You can maintain and preserve speed with this technique.

# Backward-to-Forward Transition

The backward-to-forward transition is an invaluable skill. There are numerous situations in which a seamless transition from skating backward to skating forward while staying square to your original direction of travel is needed, like when defending a rush and then having to advance for a turnover or when handling the puck backward and then advancing to make a play. The key is to maintain your momentum by not stopping in the transition.

## Method

While striding backward, start making the transition to moving forward by centering your skates together, underneath you. Bend your knees and glide backward on both skates. Turn the toe of one of your skates out 90 degrees to the direction you are traveling in; this skate will become the drive skate for the first stride of your transition to the opposite direction. Plant your skate and put pressure on the inside edge of your blade by bending your knee and leaning forward, which will allow you to angle the blade and optimize your use of its inside edge. When you thrust, rock from being on a fully flat blade to being on the ball of your foot. This movement is very similar to a forward power start (see page 44).

## Notes

It is important to maintain speed throughout your transition and to complete the transition without stopping. In order to do this, make sure that you are gliding backward on a flat blade. As well, your heels should touch when you bring your skates together as you begin the forward power start. This will stop you from stepping out of the transition, and it will help you perform a complete stride and begin the forward motion with a full extension. On the power start, the forward lean is essential to maintaining speed and even accelerating. As well, keeping the blade of the stick between your shoulders throughout this skating maneuver will help you maintain a proper body position.

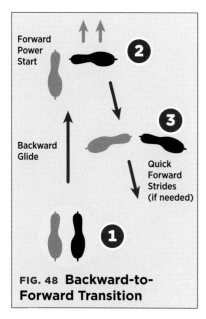

Forward Power Start

Backward Glide

Quick Forward Strides (if needed)

**FIG. 48 Backward-to-Forward Transition**

## Transition to Break Out of Zone

**1** Leaning forward helps Shea Weber make a quick transition, allowing him to use as much of the inside edges of his skates as possible. It also naturally leads the power from the transition in the right direction.

**2** He is focusing the pressure at the ball of his foot with the entire length of his blade on the ice. He will thrust from the ball of his foot to begin quickly striding.

**3** Weber turns out his foot and keeps it close to the ice for efficient, quick striding and recovery. The transition is a moving forward power start. In this instance, Weber will plant his right (same) foot and likely make a pass from that foot.

## Back-Up and Turn

This is a backward-to-forward transition (or pivot) that allows you to go from skating backward to skating forward in the same direction.

### Cross-Over Technique

Use this technique if you are skating backward and need to turn and skate forward with speed, like when chasing a player or a puck that is behind you.

While striding backward, reach one of your feet laterally to the side you wish to turn toward. Grab the ice with this skate, and, as you would in a cross-under (see page 40), draw the ice toward your body (this is like a reach and pull). As you draw the ice toward your glide skate, pivot your glide skate 90 degrees to the direction you wish to turn and rotate your upper body so you begin facing this same direction. Draw your skate underneath your body toward your glide skate and execute a cross-under behind and underneath your glide skate. Simultaneously, cross your glide skate over your cross-under skate (this is similar to a forward power start with a cross-over; see page 44). As your cross-over skate lands, begin to stride forward in your desired direction as you recover your cross-under skate for the next stride.

### Skate-to-Skate Technique

The second technique is a skate-to-skate turn, which is used to close the gap on a player who has moved laterally and is threatening to go past you.

While striding backward, reach one of your feet laterally to the side you wish to turn toward (toward the attacking player), grab the ice with this outstretched skate and draw the ice toward your body. Instead of crossing your drawing skate underneath your glide skate, pivot your glide skate 90 degrees to the direction you wish to turn, and tap your two skates together (very similar to the backward-to-forward transition). At the same time, begin to rotate your upper body so that you are facing into the turn. Stride forward beginning with your glide skate.

With the skate-to-skate technique, keep your skates near the ice at all times so you can adjust quickly to an attack move. The cross-over technique is often not suitable for closing the gap on an attacking player, as you will be unable to adjust to an attack move with your cross-over skate in the air. With both techniques be sure to quickly move your stick between your shoulders to lead you during the transition.

# Forward-to-Forward Transition

There are times during a hockey game when you will be traveling forward in one direction and will almost immediately want to go forward in the opposite direction—all while not taking your eyes off the play (or puck). If you didn't have to watch the play, you could skate forward one way, execute a tight turn and very quickly start skating forward in the other direction. But when you want to keep your eye on the puck and maintain your speed, like when a puck-side winger moves back into a break-out position in the defensive zone, you need to execute a forward-to-forward transition.

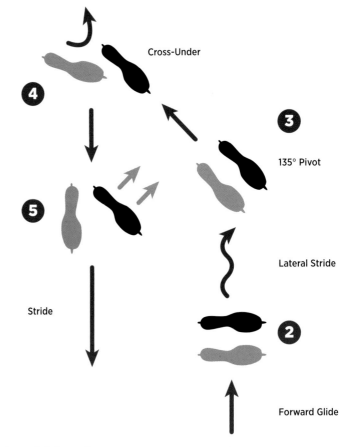

FIG. 49
**Forward-to-Forward Transition**

This is a very complicated move, mainly because while you are making the transition from forward in one direction to forward in the opposite direction you have to skate backward for a short period of time. The transition is broken into four parts, and it all starts with a lateral slide.

## Slide

The key to maintaining your speed throughout this transition is to use a lateral slide (see page 42) into the transition instead of stopping. As you are skating forward, perform the lateral slide so that you are facing your desired direction (toward the play). The slide can be straight legged initially to reduce the amount of drag on your blades and increase your speed, but as you move into the transition you will have to bend your knees in order to accelerate.

## Pivot

From your slide, pivot your heels so that you can glide backward. *Do not* pivot 180 degrees (which would send you backward on the same line you were already traveling in). Instead, pivot 135 degrees (a little less than a half-turn) so that you are traveling backward in the same general direction but on a slight angle, away from the play. Keep your skates parallel, and glide with both skates on a flat blade.

## Cross-Under

Once you are traveling backward, make your transition to go forward in the opposite direction by doing a cross-under (see page 40) followed by a stride forward. Perform the cross-under by using the back skate of your lateral slide to draw the ice toward and underneath the front skate of your lateral slide. The back skate is the cross-under skate. Remember to keep your knees bent. Rotate the cross-under skate as it passes beneath you and behind your other skate (which is gliding) so you can thrust with the outside edge of the blade at the pad of your foot. Add an ankle extension as you thrust to increase your speed.

## Stride

As the cross-under skate recovers, stride forward, starting the first stride with your original front foot. Continue to stride forward with both feet to successfully complete a forward-to-forward transition.

## Notes

The angle of the path you take when pivoting to skate backward will depend on how tight you intend the transition to be, how quickly you need to transition and how much room you have available. The less space and the quicker the desired transition, the sharper the backward angle should be. If you have a lot of space and time, the angle can be more open. Also, always keep the blade of your stick centered between your shoulders when executing the forward-to-forward transition. This will help you maintain a proper body position, balance and glide.

**Cross-Under to Forward Stride**

Mike Cammalleri is completing a forward-to-forward transition by crossing under with a full extension of his cross-under leg as he sets off in his new direction. By keeping his stick blade centered between his shoulders, he is in proper position and ready to take a pass. Forwards often need to execute a forward-to-forward transition during a breakout after a back-check.

# Lateral Skating

This technique will allow you to move laterally with speed and stability. It is used frequently, both when players are carrying the puck and when they are moving into open areas to create options for teammates. Defense often use this technique to change the point of attack when moving the puck across the blue line in the offensive zone. In the defensive or neutral zones, lateral skating can create a passing lane or space when you are being forechecked.

It is essential that you are in a position to handle the puck, shoot and pass the puck or receive a pass while moving laterally. In order to move with speed and stability, one of your skates (the glide skate) must always be on the ice while your other skate (the drive skate) draws the ice toward your glide skate. A deep knee bend is essential during this maneuver, as are vertical weight transfers, which will provide additional speed.

## Moving to the Off Side

**1** Claude Giroux's glide skate is flat, and his heel is pointing in his direction of travel. He is bending his right knee to allow him to vertically transfer his weight over his glide skate, to increase his speed.

**2** Giroux's drive skate is crossing under. To move quickly to his off side, he uses the full outside edge of his drive skate to maximize thrust.

**3** Giroux rotates his shoulders to open his body up and give him a better view of the ice. With the puck on his forehand, he is set up for a shot or pass.

**FIG. 50 Moving to Off Side**
Player shoots left and is moving laterally to the right — the off side. Position of shoulders, arms, torso and hips is very similar to skating backward. The right skate (off-side skate) drives, and the left skate (same-side skate) stays on the ice and glides.

**FIG. 51 Moving to Proper Side**
Player shoots left and is moving laterally to the left — the proper side. Shoulders, arms and torso need to be rotated to the left to keep the puck in a position where it can be passed or shot. The right skate (off-side skate) stays on the ice and glides, and the left skate (same-side skate) drives.

## Moving Toward the Off Side

This is when left-handed players move to their right and right-handed players move to their left. The drive skate is the off skate (the right skate for a left-handed player and the left skate for a right-handed player). The glide skate is the same skate. To move laterally, point the heel of your glide skate in your desired direction of travel. Next, reach and pull with your drive skate the way you would to initiate a cross-under, drawing the ice toward your glide skate with the inside edge of the entire blade of your drive skate. Draw the ice repeatedly with quick strokes, and execute your cross-unders with a quick recovery with your drive skate. Your glide skate stays on the ice on a flat blade.

When traveling toward the off side, your body should be positioned almost as if you were moving backward, similar to the technique used to skate backward around a curve.

## Moving Toward the Proper Side

This is when left-handed players move to their left and right-handed players move to their right. Now the glide skate is the off skate (the right skate for a left-handed player and the left skate for a right-handed player). The drive skate is the same skate. The technique to move laterally to the proper side is the same as to move laterally to the off side. Keep in mind, however, that when moving to the proper side, your upper body has to be rotated to remain square so you can shoot or pass the puck at any time. Your upper body should be opened up to be 90 degrees to your direction of travel. This is a very challenging skill to master. Players who can acquire this skill can pick up pucks on their off side at the boards along the blue line in the offensive zone (on their backhand), and they can then move laterally across the blue line toward the middle of the rink for a shot or a pass.

# Tight Turns

A tight turn is a great tool to use to create space or close a gap. Offensively, you can use a tight turn to evade players, maintain puck possession or release from a checker to get open. Defensively, the ability to turn tightly will allow you to maintain a good defensive position and take away the space of your opponent.

## Tight Turn to the Forehand

1. Sidney Crosby's stick blade enters the turn first, followed by his inside skate and his outside skate. He is cupping his stick blade to control the puck on his forehand.

2. Crosby brings his top hand across his body and underneath the forearm of his bottom hand to allow his stick blade to cup the puck and lead the turn. Crosby uses a short stick. If he used a longer stick, he would have to place his hand much further under his forearm to achieve the same result.

3. Crosby thrusts through the turn with his heels — on the outside edge of his blade on his lead foot and the inside edge of his blade on his trailing foot. Crosby glides through the turn with the rest of his skate blade (on each foot) in contact with the ice, maximizing his speed on the turn.

4. Crosby's lean into the turn toward the goal seals off the defender and gives him a clear path to the net.

## Entering the Turn

When you enter a tight turn, you need to be in the hockey-playing position. Extend the skate that will be on the inside of the turn forward with a flat blade and lean your body in that direction, keeping your knee over the extended foot with a forward body lean. You should be using the outside edge of your inside skate and the inside edge of your outside skate. Enter the turn with your stick blade first, then with your inside knee/skate and then with your outside skate. You can determine the path of your turn by the way you position your lead skate. The tighter the turn, the closer your lead skate should be to your body and the more you need to bend your lead leg. The more gradual the turn, the further your lead skate should be from your body. To generate more speed on the turn, thrust with a heel push from your back foot. Keeping your feet on the same trajectory also enhances speed.

## Through the Turn

Keep your top hand away from your body on the backhand and across your body and underneath the forearm of your bottom arm on the forehand. This promotes glide and puck control. Rotate the top hand to cup the puck. Drive the inside knee forward and use a heel push from your outside skate to maintain speed, or even accelerate, through the turn.

## Exiting the Turn

As you come to the end of your turn, increase your speed by driving your inside knee forward, moving it further over and in front of your lead skate. This will keep your body low to the ice, help protect the puck and, most importantly, maximize your glide. To come out of the tight turn with speed, use a heel push off your back skate. Then, thrust off the inside edge at the ball of your foot and cross this skate over your lead skate. As your back skate crosses over, cross-under with your lead skate. An elite player can reach forward with his lead skate and draw the ice toward himself before he executes a strong cross-under (and ankle extension) with his lead skate—which catapults him into a drive out of the tight turn. After your tight turn, try moving forward laterally with a few quick cross-over/under combos.

## Slowing Down

If you are going too fast when you are entering a turn and need to slow yourself down in order to execute the turn effectively, rotate your lead skate and thrust it laterally in your direction of travel (with your toes facing into the turn and your heel facing away from the turn). The inside arch of your foot should be facing away from you so you can use the outside edge of your skate (the edge closest to your body) to scrape the ice with a flat, lateral blade.

**FIG. 52**

### Tight Turn to the Forehand

**Top hand is brought across the body and underneath the forearm of the bottom hand to allow the stick blade to cup the puck and lead the turn, keeping the blade close to the lead foot. Knee is thrust ahead of the lead skate to protect the puck and to increase the weight over the lead skate, adding glide to the turn.**

**FIG. 53**

### Tight Turn to the Backhand

**Top hand is held up and away from the body and bottom hand is stretched across the body to keep the stick close to the lead foot. Knee is thrust over the lead skate to protect the puck and to increase the weight over and in front of the lead skate, adding glide to the turn.**

# Drive and Delay

In some quarters this technique is called the Bobby Orr escape move, as No. 4 made the drive and delay a part of his regular on-ice repertoire. In a drive and delay, you accelerate on a curve in one direction—drive—and then quickly turn in a tight glide away from the path of the original turn—delay. This technique creates space and is used in many situations: driving the net with the puck only to be cut off by a defensive player then delaying to create space and options, driving over the blue line into the offensive zone and then delaying toward the boards, or avoiding forecheckers in your own zone by driving toward your own net and then delaying into the corner.

## Drive

The driving part of this technique is simple. Accelerate by using the forward cross-over technique (see page 36) to make a strong drive on a curve.

## Delay

When you have reached the point when you want to delay, you need to go from crossing over to a tight turn. To do this, you need to drive off the inside edge of your cross-over skate (your outside skate) the same as you would for a cross-over, but before your skate crosses over and contacts the ice, you need to rotate your foot away from your initial direction of travel so that your foot will be facing your new direction of travel. The inside arch of your foot should be facing away from you, and when you plant your foot on the ice, your skate should be angled so that you are using your outside edge (also known as an outside-edge reverse). This skate will become your lead skate for the tight turn.

Once you are on the outside edge of your lead skate, bring your other foot (your inside skate on the cross-over) around to follow your lead foot. This foot will now become your outside skate in the tight turn, and it will be your drive skate. As in a tight turn, you will drive off the inside edge of the heel of the outside skate to maintain speed or even accelerate through the turn.

## Notes

When you initiate the delay, ensure that you are in a deep knee bend, with the knee of your lead leg driving forward. This gives you the proper positioning to maximize glide on the tight turn and to create space. It is critical that you position your hands properly through the cross-overs and then quickly change their position when moving into the delay. This will help you maintain speed and even accelerate. It will also help you control and protect the puck.

## Delay to the Corner

1. Lee Stempniak was initially moving to his backhand. He is using an outside-edge reverse with his left foot to suddenly change direction to his forehand by driving the outside edge of his left blade into the ice. His right foot will follow his left foot as his stick blade leads toward his new direction in a tight turn to the forehand.

2. Stempniak has moved his top hand in toward his body, and as he continues his tight turn to the forehand, he'll further push his top hand under the forearm of his bottom hand in order to help him execute the turn.

3. Stempniak will drive with the inside edge of his right foot and accelerate through a tight turn (see page 84) to delay to his forehand and separate from the defender.

# Heel-to-Heel Turn

Skating heel to heel allows you to open up and face into a turn while handling the puck. It is very effective when executing wraparounds, as it allows you to open up, accelerate using the thrust of the trailing skate and see the position of the goalie and defenders. It also makes you a constant threat through the turn, as you are always in a position to pass or shoot the puck, even though you are turning. When you don't have the puck, a heel-to-heel turn is an excellent way to move efficiently and directly in a tight space.

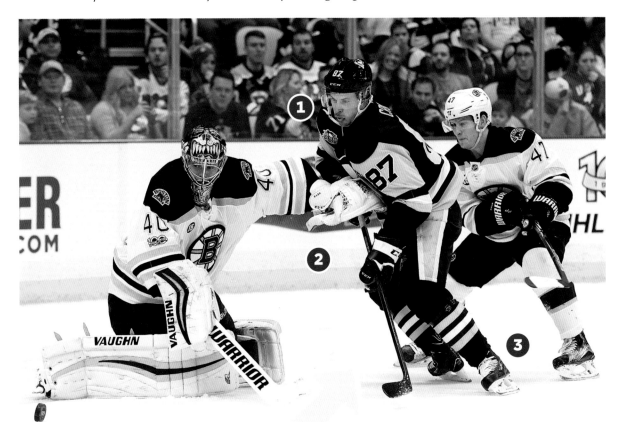

## Heel-to-Heel Turn in a Tight Space

**1** Sidney Crosby's forward body lean keeps him on the inside edge of both of his skates.

**2** In this tight space, Crosby's heel-to-heel turn allows him to stay square to the loose puck while accelerating quickly and directly to the puck.

**3** He is generating thrust from the inside edge of his right (trailing) skate at the ball of his foot, sending him on a curve to his left (forehand). The heel of his drive skate glides, as does his entire left (lead) skate. He is bending his knees to transfer his weight vertically, achieved by rocking on his skates. Crosby can quickly separate from the defender while keeping his body between the defender and the puck. Upon reaching the puck, Crosby's heel-to-heel turn will keep him square to the net for a scoring chance.

## Method

To execute a heel-to-heel turn, you need to open your hips and rotate both of your skates so your toes face out and your heels are together. Your lead skate should point toward your direction of travel, and your trailing skate should point toward the direction you came from. The gap between your skates can be from a hand width to shoulder width apart, with the wider stance being more stable. To ensure proper glide, and even acceleration, you need to use a deep knee bend with vertical weight transfers, as well as thrusts from the inside edges of both skates (from the ball of the trailing foot and the heel of the lead foot). Make sure the angle of your skates allows you to use your inside edges. The main thrust on the turn should come from the ball of your trailing skate. Your glide is generated on the heel of your trailing skate and on the entire blade of your front skate.

## Notes

Turning heel to heel is generally more gradual than a tight turn. Some players will alternate between a tight turn and a heel-to-heel turn when carrying the puck. A tight turn will put you in a better position to protect the puck if there is pressure, while the heel-to-heel turn puts you in a better position to open up and see more of the ice to make a play. Generally, players use the heel-to-heel turn to move to their forehand. Advanced players add vertical weight transfers to the turn to increase the thrust they are generating by "rocking" their skates—bending their knees and moving their ankles up and down to put added pressure on the ball of the trailing foot and the heel of the lead foot. This can be particularly effective when using the heel-to-heel turn for a wraparound.

**FIG. 54 Deep Bend**

**With your knees deeply bent you get more pressure on your edges, which can be turned into speed and power when you use vertical weight transfers and thrusts from the ball of your lead foot and the heel of your trailing foot. A deep knee bend also allows your hands to be closer to the ice, enabling you to push the puck further away from you as you slide your bottom hand toward your top hand. The extended reach coupled with the powerful drive makes this an excellent option for a wraparound from behind the net.**

# Fake Shots

Faking a shot and moving to your forehand is an easy way to add deception to your game. When faking a shot it is important to imitate the shooting motion as closely as possible; the defender has to believe you are going to shoot the puck in order for the fake to work.

## Fake Shot

**1** Connor McDavid's head is up and his eyes are looking at the target to help sell the fake.

**2** With the puck on his forehand side in a position to pass or shoot, McDavid transfers his weight to his off foot. As he moves his weight to his off foot, he can simultaneously flex his stick with his bottom hand to help further sell the fake to the defender.

**3** McDavid could shoot at this point, but he could also move his top hand away from his body, fake the shot and drive off the fake, as shown in Fig. 56.

## Fake Slap Shot

This is the easiest fake shot to learn. While effective on its own, it is also a stepping-stone that will help you learn more challenging dekes and learn to move laterally to your forehand off a fake.

To sell the shot, bring your stick back to initiate the slap-shot motion. Move your stick quickly through the shooting motion, moving your hands across and in toward your body as the blade moves toward the puck. Simultaneously bring your same foot (back foot) under your body and toward your off foot. Keep your same foot close to the ice. Progressively bend both of your knees and bring your same foot underneath your body to touch your off foot. When your stick blade reaches the puck, stop the forward motion of your hands: push your top hand away from your body and bring your bottom hand into your body while rolling your wrists to rotate the stick blade so it is open and facing your forehand side. The puck will be on your forehand side and your blade will be facing the direction you are going to drive off the fake, not the original direction of your "shot." Take a full stride to your forehand side, driving from your off foot and leading with your same foot. The angle on which you accelerate to beat the defender or create space will depend on many factors, including your speed and the positioning and reaction of the defender.

**FIG. 55**

### Fake Slap-Shot Windup

**Wind up for your fake shot as you would for a regular slap shot, but keep in mind that the longer your stick is in the air behind you, the more time you are giving to defenders to close the gap on you. A short to medium backswing is best.**

## Fake Snap Shot

You sell a fake off-foot snap shot by going through exactly the same motions you do for a fake slap shot, except your backswing for the snap shot is not as large. This makes the fake snap shot less pronounced than the fake slap shot, and in order to effectively sell the snap shot you need to exaggerate the body and hand movements outlined for the fake slap shot (but with a smaller backswing). It also means that you don't have as much time to bring your same foot underneath you in order to set up your drive off the fake, so you need to be very quick.

You can also fake a snap shot by keeping your stick blade on the ice. This fake is subtler and again requires that you exaggerate your body and hand movements to sell the shot. Your foot and hand movements are the same as those previously described. However, your stick movement at the outset of the fake snap shot is different.

Start with the puck out slightly ahead of you on your forehand side and extend your reach. Fake the snap shot by rolling your wrists to lift the heel of your stick off the

### FIG. 56 Drive off the Fake

**As your stick blade nears the puck (the point just before you would release it if you were shooting), rotate your wrists, push your top hand out and turn your blade to face your forehand side. Lean into the drive and push to your forehand side with your off foot (the front foot in your original shooting motion).**

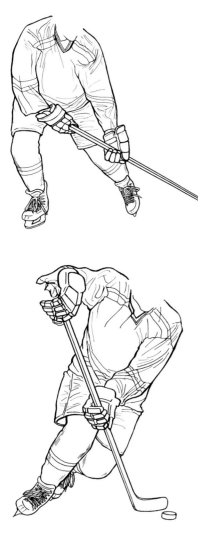

**FIG. 57 & 58 Snap-Shot Fake to Forehand Drive**
Start with the puck on your forehand side out from your body. With a toe drag, cradle the puck and drag it toward your feet with the heel of your stick in the air. Have your eyes up looking at your "shot target." Simultaneously bring your same-side foot underneath your body, beside your off foot. Rotate your wrists, push your top hand out and turn your blade to face your forehand side. Lean into the drive and push to your forehand side with your off foot.

ice and, with the toe of your stick, drag the puck in toward your body. As you drag the puck in toward your body, roll your wrists in the opposite direction so that the heel of your stick returns to the ice. You'll need to move your top hand out and away from your body as your same foot comes underneath you in preparation for your lateral drive to your forehand, just as you do during the fake slap shot. When you are in this position, which looks identical to the position of the fake slap shot, take a full stride to your forehand, driving off your off foot and leading with your same foot. This fake can be very effective because the puck moves quite a bit through the shooting motion, an extra element the defender needs to read.

## Fake Wrist Shot

The movement for this fake is the subtlest of all the off-foot fake shots, and it requires you commit to exaggerating the movements of your wrist shot.

The same general technique used for the fake slap shot is used for the fake wrist shot, except the puck remains on your stick at all times. Sell the fake by bringing the puck back as you would for a wrist shot and then quickly bring it forward as though you are going to release the shot. As you bring the puck forward on your fake shot, bring your hands into your body. As you reach what would ordinarily be the point of release, push your top hand out and away from your body and bring your

bottom hand into your body while rolling your wrists to rotate the stick blade so it is open and facing your forehand side—the same way you would for the fake slap shot and the fake snap shot. As with the slap-shot and snap-shot fakes, you need to simultaneously bring your same foot underneath you and toward your off foot so you can quickly drive off your fake to the forehand.

If you start your fake wrist shot with the puck away from your body, you can use a toe drag to keep the puck on your stick and move your hands into your body to begin setting up the drive —same as you would a fake snap shot.

The real challenge of the fake wrist shot is to bring the puck forward quickly enough to sell the shot and then slow the puck down, rotate your top hand and quickly drive laterally to your forehand side while keeping the puck under control the entire time.

## Fake Backhand Shot

Like a slap shot or wrist shot, you can fake a backhand shot and move off the fake to a forehand position for a shot, a pass or a drive into open space. One difficulty with the fake backhand is that in selling the backhand shot you have to drop your head just before the "shot," making yourself vulnerable to a defender who might step up to make contact. It is important to give yourself enough space from the defender when you initiate the fake and to move quickly between the shooting fake and the forehand position.

**FIG. 59** **Fake Backhand Setup**
Place the puck behind your off foot, the same way you would if you were setting up a backhand shot. To help sell the shot, drop your same-side shoulder and, if it is safe to do so, you can briefly drop your head.

**FIG. 60** **Transition from Shot to Turn**
Sweep the puck forward and drive from the inside edge of your off foot and the outside edge of your same foot to initiate a tight turn. Cup the puck on the back of your blade and in close to your feet to avoid stick checks. Progress through the turn, and once on your forehand side, lift your stick over the puck so that it is on the forehand side of your stick blade.

Set up the fake backhand shot as you would a real backhand, with your same side closest to the target. Have your stick blade square to the target and back of center with the puck cradled on the back of your blade. Lower your same-side shoulder to further sell the shot, and if safe to do so, drop your head. Sweep your hands forward as you would if you were releasing the shot, but instead, bring your hands in toward and across your body to your forehand side, keeping the puck on the back of your blade. Simultaneously drive from the inside edge of your off foot and the outside edge of your same foot to rotate your feet with your body. The motion of your stick, body and feet is very similar to executing a tight turn on your backhand. Once you have turned to your forehand side, lift your stick blade over the puck to the front of your blade so you are ready to shoot or pass on the forehand.

This can be a great fake on a goaltender, especially when combined with a move back to your backhand after initially faking the backhand shot and moving to your forehand (a double fake). Make sure you give yourself extra room to execute the two moves.

### Same-Foot Fake Shot

Same-foot fakes have become much more common as the use of same-foot shots has increased. If you are faking a wrist shot or snap shot off your same foot, or off both of your feet, you can move effectively to your forehand or to your backhand off the fake.

To sell a same-foot fake, set up as if you are going to take the shot. Lean your body to your same side and apply lots of pressure to the shaft of your stick with your bottom hand. Raise, or raise and kick, your off foot, as this gives the impression that you have committed to the shot.

In most cases, in order to move to your forehand or backhand side off the fake, you have to bring your off foot back down on the ice. However, the split-second hesitation that raising your foot can buy you is often enough to get a defender or the goalie out of position long enough for you to capitalize on their mistake. Once you have frozen the defending player, you can put your off foot down and attack laterally on your forehand or backhand side.

It is also very effective to hesitate in the shooting position after you have brought your off foot back onto the ice and are still square to the defender or goalie. This gives you a second opportunity to freeze the defending player and may buy you more time to execute your move to your backhand or forehand side. Any time you have pressure on your stick with your blade facing a target and your shoulders square to the net, you are a threat to shoot.

**FIG. 61 & 62**

## Changing the Angle of Attack

Fake a same-foot shot and hold the fake as long as you can in order to freeze the defender. Lean slightly toward your same side and use the outside edge of your same-side blade to turn toward your forehand side, giving you a new angle to shoot or pass the puck. To execute the move with speed, pump your off-side knee as you turn toward your forehand side.

## Notes on Fake Shots

### Keys to the Forehand Drive off the Fake

Once you fake a shot you are in position to accelerate off the fake, but be quick, as the window of opportunity is small. After your initial drive — pushing from your off foot and leading with your same leg — you must accelerate using cross-overs and drive around your opponent into open space. Your drive can lead you to the net or, against good defenders who adjust to the fake quickly, you can use a drive and delay to create space. You can also shoot or pass off the fake before the defender has time to either adjust and fill the shooting lane or get a stick on your stick as you are shooting.

### To Shoot or Not to Shoot

With all fake shots, you can wait to decide whether or not to shoot until just before the point of release. This will help you "sell" your shot, since you can actually be in the process of shooting then decide that it will be to your advantage — due to the positioning of the defender or the goalie or other factors — to fake the shot instead.

### Using Fake Shots to Change Angles

Faking a shot (or even just hesitating while in a shooting position) in order to freeze the defender or goalie, or to have the defender or goalie commit to the fake, is a great play, giving you time and space to make a play or to move the puck to a different shooting position. The key to changing the angle or

## Options off the Same-Foot Fake

✳ You can use use the fake same-foot shot as a fake dump-in to create space in front of you. For example, if you are attacking a defender through the neutral zone on your off wing, the fake dump-in off your same foot may cause the defender to back off a little, giving you more space to work.

✳ It is possible to deke to your forehand side before you put your off foot onto the ice, but you should not use this fake to get around an opponent; instead, you should use it to change the angle of your shot or pass. To execute this fake, raise your off foot from the ice as you would for a same-foot shot. Once you are in this position, begin to turn toward your forehand side by using the outside edge of your same skate—lean in slightly toward the puck using your stick for balance. To give yourself a boost of speed, pump the knee of your off leg (which is already in the air) by thrusting it up and into your body. This will propel you on your same foot toward your forehand side. Once you have changed the angle, look to quickly shoot or pass the puck. Keith Tkachuk has used this fake very effectively.

---

shooting position is to move the puck from the release position of the "intended" shot to the new shooting position as quickly as possible before releasing the puck. Your new shooting position may mean moving the puck a short distance or a long distance, but either way it will change the angle of the shot. In order to release the shot as quickly as possible, you may need to shoot off an extended reach, either on your backhand or your forehand side, or you may need to shoot from a position with the puck drawn into your body.

You can effectively use many different shots off this fake, and because so many goalies are very good at covering the bottom of the net while moving laterally, it is to your advantage to put the puck high after moving it to your new shooting point. This fake is effective whether you are in close to the goalie or farther out. The open-bladed shot (see page 71), which allows you to get the puck up quickly, is particularly effective in this situation. If you want to keep the puck low to the ice, try a low, hard shot to the five-hole, as many goalies open up their five-hole when they move laterally to adjust to the change in the shooting angle. If you have used your fake in close to the goalkeeper, your best option may be to shoot with one hand off an extended reach. This will often result in a tap-in after you have moved the puck back against the direction in which both you and the goalie are traveling (see the Forsberg move, page 120). Changing your shooting angle is a very effective move on breakaways and shootouts.

## Double Fakes

A double fake can create open space, but it requires room, as you need to fake a shot and then fake a drive to your forehand side, only to come back and drive around the defender to your backhand side. To do this, fake a shot and drive to your forehand side. Once you have begun your forehand drive, quickly move the puck across your body toward your backhand side. Continue pushing the puck to your backhand side while extending your reach and using cross-overs to accelerate into a backhand drive. The key is to use the momentum you gained from your first fake to accelerate into the drive for your second fake. Remember to start your first fake earlier to give yourself more space between you and the defender in order to execute the two fakes.

# The Hidden Shot

Adapted from the European sport of floorball, the hidden shot is yet another way to get a puck off quickly with minimal detection. With this technique, you can momentarily conceal the puck from the goaltender, create separation from a blocking defender and disguise the release point, making it difficult for the goalie to follow the puck and predict when and where you will take the shot.

## The Hidden Shot

**1** After faking to his backhand side and then moving to his forehand side, Alex Ovechkin pulls the puck back, rotating his body from the net. He shoots the puck with a sweeping motion that started from beside his same foot and ends with a release of the puck, just as it clears his off foot. The off foot conceals the puck until he releases the shot. Ovechkin further obscures his shot by using the defenseman as a screen.

**2** Ovechkin's torso and shoulders have rotated during the sweeping motion he used to move the puck from beside his same foot and across his entire body. His rotation is further pronounced because of his full and high follow-through.

**3** Ovechkin's same foot leaves the ice to allow his body to twist and complete the follow-through of the shot.

## Method

The hidden shot is best set up with the puck on your forehand. Execute a heel turn followed by a lateral drive on your forehand to begin working around your defender. Next, execute a toe drag to bring the puck close to your body and between you and your defender, effectively concealing the puck while you are gliding with your skates pointed in the direction you are moving. You then step your off foot forward and move it further away from your defender in the direction you are gliding. With your weight transferred to your off foot, you can quickly sweep the puck into a forehand shooting position in front of your off foot. That foot will further conceal the puck through the sweeping shooting motion, and you can release the puck with a wrist shot with your weight on your off foot as soon as the puck clears that skate. Another option is to sweep the puck into shooting position and drive your same foot in the same direction, with a quick cross-over step, before shooting off your same foot. The advantage is that the cross-over step or steps will create further separation between you and your defender, allowing you to avoid a defending stick, and create more movement during the shot for the goalie to deal with. The disadvantage is that, after being concealed, the puck will be exposed longer before you shoot. One of the very best at the hidden shot is Russian sniper Vladamir Taresenko.

## Tip

Practice your move using two stationary cones set up at different distances from each other and from the net. One cone represents the initial position of a defender, and the second cone represents the position as the defender tries to follow you. The key is to execute your lateral move to your forehand and the toe drag of the puck at the first cone and then glide laterally between the cones while you are concealing and protecting the puck. As your approach the second cone, sweep the puck quickly to a shooting position before releasing it with your weight either on your off foot or your same foot using the shooting-in-motion technique.

When executed properly, your speed will change throughout the move, and you will slow down during the heel turn before the lateral move and then accelerate just before the shot. Some players will also use a toe drag during the initial lateral move before pushing their top hand away from their body, pushing the puck to their forehand side and then toe dragging the puck back to conceal it with their body. The hidden shot is set up by a combination of a number of moves. It is a challenge but well worth the time you will spend learning it!

# Knee-Down Shot

A knee-down shot expands your wheelhouse—the area your range of stick motion allows you to reliably and accurately strike the puck for a shot—and allows you to convert a poor pass or rebound into a great scoring opportunity, especially when you are in tight to the net.

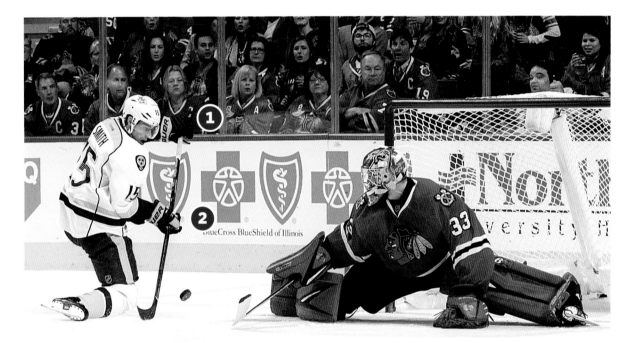

## Knee-Down Shot for a Rebound Opportunity

**1** Craig Smith's top hand is up and away from his body so he can keep his stick blade square to the ice while dropping to his same knee. His rotates his wrist slightly to open his blade, so that when he shoots, he can lift the puck high, over the sprawling goalie.

**2** While he waits for the rebound, he rotates the wrist on his bottom hand and brings his elbow close to his hip in order to bring his stick blade in close to his leg on the ice. This give's Smith the maximum amount of space possible to get his shot up once he corrals the loose puck.

## Technique

To execute a knee-down shot, drop down on your same knee and bend your off knee while raising the top hand on your stick and keeping your stick blade square to the ice. As you go to shoot, keep your bottom hand low on the shaft of your stick, which will allow you to get your blade on pucks that are in close to your body and give your shot accuracy and power.

Players often use this shot when they are set up on their off side and a pass they want to release quickly

**Shooting Sooner**

Mika Zibanejad fires a knee-down shot in an attempt to move the puck to the net sooner and from a better angle than he could if he were to receive his pass and fire his shot from his feet. Getting the puck to the net quicker means the goalie has less time to react and get set. The goalie may open holes as he moves quickly from one side of the net to the other, increasing Zibanejad's chance of scoring.

toward the net is directed ahead of them. The knee-down shot allows you to one-time the puck with your blade squarer to the puck than if you were to remain on your feet. Even a pass that is well in front of you can be one-timed with a quick step forward and a drop to one knee. Choking down on the shaft of your stick in order to keep the blade square to the puck will increase this shot's accuracy, as you have more control over the direction of the puck when you strike it with a short swing. Some players like to use the knee-down

shot to get the puck up quickly on opportunities in tight to the net when the goalie is covering the low part of the goal.

**Tip**

Practice passing the puck with a partner who is also in a knee-down position, making sure your top hand is away from your body and your stick blade is square to the ice. Deliberately try to pass the puck ahead of your partner's skates. Next, try to expand the area in which you are able to receive and return a pass with your knee

down. Then set yourself up in a knee-down position near the net toward your off-side post and have your partner throw some pucks into and ahead of your skates. Try converting these passes into one-time shots, and see how quickly you can get the puck up. Finally, try converting passes while standing upright and dropping into the knee-down position. Have your partner steadily increase the speed of the passes so you can practice quickly moving from an upright position to a knee-down one.

# Shooting Between Your Legs

Drawing the puck between your legs and taking a forehand shot is no longer just for show-offs! Shooting between your legs is now recognized as an effective way to protect the puck while changing the shooting angle. It also places the puck in a position where the shooter can quickly get it up high, especially in areas where the shooter doesn't have a lot of room to operate.

One space on the ice where this move can be really effective is on a player's off-side post, beside the net and above the goal line. When in that spot, you can retrieve or receive a puck below the goal line, draw it between your legs to a shooting position above the goal line and release it on your forehand. Drawing the puck between your legs helps protect it from a poke check and disguises your shot's release point. You can move your same foot toward the goalie or the defender to give yourself more room between your legs and increase this protected area—you should bend your knee as you do this to give yourself even more space.

As you shoot, extend your arms away from your body so that you can keep your stick blade square to the ice through the shot. Players commonly execute this shot with both feet planted on the ice and with their weight evenly

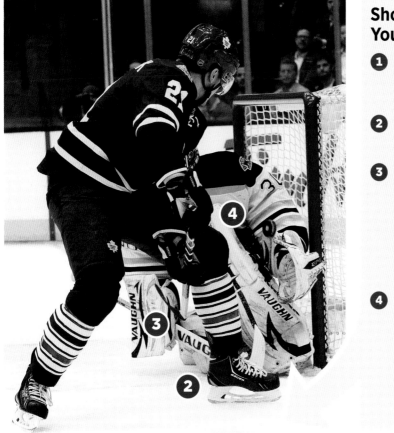

## Shooting Between Your Legs

**1** James van Riemsdyk draws the puck from the goal line and will bring it between his legs for a shot on his forehand.

**2** Van Riemsdyk turns his same foot out and rotates his shoulders and chest toward the goal.

**3** Van Riemsdyk pulls the puck from between his legs to the front of the net, moving the puck, in one motion, from in front of his body through his body and to the far side of his same foot. This dramatically changes the shooting angle and gives van Riemsdyk a much better chance on goal.

**4** Van Riemsdyk's hands rotate his stick to open the blade so that he can elevate the puck quickly in a tight space. By keeping his hands low, he creates more room to make the shooting motion between his legs, improving his ability to elevate the puck.

distributed on both feet. To get the puck up quickly, you can combine this with a knee-down shot.

### Tip

Practice drawing the puck from your off side to your proper side through your legs until you can do it quickly and under control.

Extending your arms away from your body before you draw or drag the puck will help increase the distance you move the puck before you shoot it. Extending your arms after you draw the puck through your legs will help you get your stick blade square for the shot and ensure that you clear your skates

before you release the puck. Use a cone as a stand-in for the defender or goalie, and draw the puck from your off side, through your legs to your proper side before shooting it past the cone.

# Toe Drags

A toe drag, particularly the forehand toe drag, is one of the most commonly used vertical dekes. The goal is to push the puck out, away from your body, then bring it back in. When executed properly, the toe drag allows you to move the puck a great distance from your body (enticing defenders to take the bait) before drawing it back into your body to protect it. Toe drags are very effective when coupled with lateral attack moves.

## Forehand Toe Drag

**1** Filip Forsberg has slightly extended his reach and has pushed the puck out to his forehand side. He is gliding on both skates and is in the midst of transfering his weight to his off side.

**2** Forsberg has rolled the wrist of his top hand to lift the heel of his stick blade off the ice. As Forsberg transfers his weight to his off side, he will bring the puck in close to his same-side skate by dragging it in with the toe of his stick blade and moving his top hand across his body.

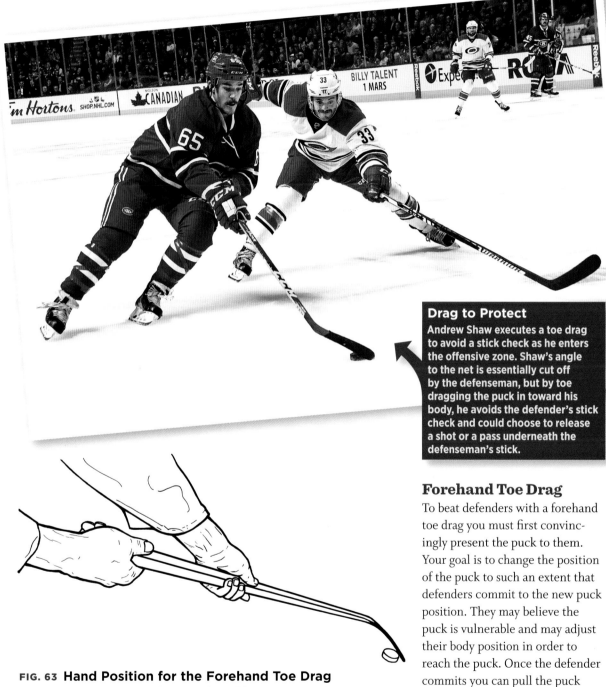

**Drag to Protect**

Andrew Shaw executes a toe drag to avoid a stick check as he enters the offensive zone. Shaw's angle to the net is essentially cut off by the defenseman, but by toe dragging the puck in toward his body, he avoids the defender's stick check and could choose to release a shot or a pass underneath the defenseman's stick.

**FIG. 63 Hand Position for the Forehand Toe Drag**

With the puck at the inside of the toe of your blade, rotate your hands so the toe of your blade becomes squarer to the ice and the heel is in the air. The back of your blade should face your opponent. Place your thumbs on the side of the shaft for better control as you drag the puck back.

## Forehand Toe Drag

To beat defenders with a forehand toe drag you must first convincingly present the puck to them. Your goal is to change the position of the puck to such an extent that defenders commit to the new puck position. They may believe the puck is vulnerable and may adjust their body position in order to reach the puck. Once the defender commits you can pull the puck back and drive to open space.

Begin by pushing the puck away from your body, either in front of

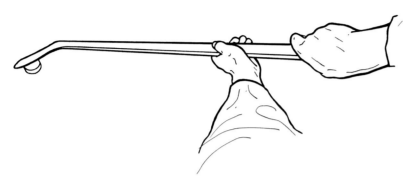

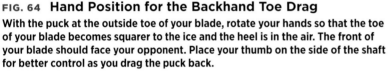

**FIG. 64  Hand Position for the Backhand Toe Drag**
With the puck at the outside toe of your blade, rotate your hands so that the toe of your blade becomes squarer to the ice and the heel is in the air. The front of your blade should face your opponent. Place your thumb on the side of the shaft for better control as you drag the puck back.

you or to your forehand side, while executing a forehand attack (lateral or straight ahead). When the defender reacts to the presentation of the puck, pull the puck back by dragging it toward you with the inside toe of your stick blade, which should be almost square to the ice; the heel of your stick should be in the air, and the back of your blade should be facing the defender. For extra control on the drag, place your thumb on the side of your stick's shaft. Next draw your hands in toward your body to pull the puck back. You can then drive around the defender, either by moving the puck across your body to your backhand side where you can execute a lateral attack to your backhand or moving back to your forehand with a lateral attack to your forehand side.

To drive to your forehand side off a forehand toe drag, bring your same foot underneath you as you draw the puck toward your body,

then drive off your off foot while extending your reach to your forehand side, just as you would during the lateral attack to your forehand.

Regardless of whether you choose to attack to your backhand or forehand side, you will want to bring your feet underneath you to allow for an effective drive and a good first stride into the lateral attack.

## Backhand Toe Drag

For the backhand toe drag, extend your reach and present the puck to the defender on your backhand side. With both hands on your stick, drag the puck in toward your body with the toe of the back of your stick blade, which should be almost square to the ice. The heel of your stick should be in the air, and the front of the blade should be facing the defender.

As you are pulling the puck in, set yourself up for a drive around

the defender. You can move the puck from your backhand side across your body to your same side for a forehand drive, or you can go back to your off side for a backhand drive. Remember to bring your feet together for an effective drive and a good first stride to the lateral attack.

## One-Handed Backhand Toe Drag

The same principles that apply to conventional two-handed drags—present the puck then drag it back and drive around the defender—apply to the one-handed backhand toe drag, except that you are presenting the puck and dragging it back with only your top hand on your stick.

Extend your reach with the puck with one hand on your stick and present it toward your backhand side. Keep your top hand and arm raised while you extend your reach to control the puck. When the defender reacts to the presentation of the puck, drag it in toward you with the backhand-side toe of your stick's blade.

You'll find it easier to drive around the defender if you sell the one-handed backhand toe drag as a backhand lateral attack move. Start by accelerating to your backhand side with one hand on your stick, and sell the defender on your intention to continue this drive. Once the defender has committed to this path, decelerate and draw the puck back with a one-handed backhand toe drag. At this point

**FIG. 65 One-Handed Backhand Toe Drag**
With one hand on your stick, practice extending your reach to the backhand with the puck, toe dragging the puck back to your backhand side, and pushing the puck back out again. Your wrist should roll more than 180 degrees from your extension to your toe drag, to the puck at your side. Remember to always keep your hand up in order to have your stick blade (and toe during the drag) square to the ice.

you can bring the puck across your body to your forehand side and drive around the defender to your forehand, or you can drag the puck back and drive again to your backhand side.

To drive back to your backhand side, drag the puck in toward you with the backhand-side toe of your stick's blade. As the puck moves toward you, the back of your stick blade will be facing you and your palm will be facing down. Once you bring your top hand into your body, rotate your top hand so that your palm is facing up and your stick blade moves between you and the puck. The puck will still be on the back of your blade. Next,

quickly push the puck ahead of you and to your backhand side with the back of your blade. Accelerate and continue the drive to your backhand side. This option can get defenders tied up, and it should give you enough room after the toe drag to beat the player to the backhand.

## Keys to the Toe Drag

Toe drags often work well with an acceleration to set them up and then a deceleration as the drag is being executed. Extending your arms just before you slow down will make your presentation of the puck more pronounced and give you more room to drag the puck back. The idea is to accelerate forward with the puck and then decelerate while extending your reach, which you use to continue the forward movement of the puck even though you have stopped skating forward. This will disguise your deceleration, making it more likely for the defender to be caught out of position. Some players have had success with this move when on their proper side on a 1-on-1 or a 2-on-1. In this instance, the defender will angle toward the puck carrier hoping to block a shot or pass. The puck carrier can use deceleration combined with a toe drag to change the angle of attack, leaving the defender out of position and creating space for a shot or a pass.

# Shooting in Motion

Shooting in motion is one of the most effective ways to disguise the release point of your shot and, hopefully, catch a goaltender napping. Shooting in motion is an excellent tactic when you have a clear path to the net, but it is even better if you can use a defender as a screen to further disguise your release of the puck.

## Shooting Through a Defender

**1** As he approaches a defender, Artem Anisimov keeps the puck away from his body and in a shooting position. Before shooting in motion, he raises the heel of his stick in order to pull the puck toward his same foot, thereby changing the shooting angle. His drag to change the angle will move seamlessly into a snap shot from beside his same foot. The faster Anisimov can make this motion, the better the odds the goaltender will not have adjusted to his new shooting angle.

**2** Anisimov can use the defender as a screen for the goalie, further disguising his drag to change the angle and his shot.

Typically, shooting in motion refers to shooting the puck at the net with a forehand shot while performing cross-overs. With traditional shooting, players stop skating before shooting in order to transfer the weight from the back foot to the front foot when releasing the puck. This allows the goalie to prepare for the shot, squaring to the shooter and even advancing to take away visible net. When you shoot in motion, the goalie may not be expecting the shot and will likely also be in motion—and not set—for your release.

## Technique

The best way to shoot in motion is to shoot off of your same foot. This release should come when your full weight has been transferred to your same foot and you are driving off that skate as you do cross-overs. To shoot the puck, your hands should be pushed forward, but brought into the body just before you shoot to put as much weight as possible on the stick when releasing the puck. Sometimes a slight toe drag of the puck to bring it a little closer to you before you release will help you control the path of the puck and maximize the power in your shot. Your head should always be up so that you can look for openings and watch how the goalie is reacting. Shooting in motion can be used in many situations, including off a fake and a drive around a defender, when driving the net from your proper side or when moving to the middle of the ice from the half boards.

## Tip

Place a cone in front of the net between the inside hash marks on the circle and the face-off dot. Starting at the goal line, skate to the cone with a puck. Do a tight cross-over turn around the cone to your forehand side and drive toward the net. Release the puck in motion off your same foot just after you round the cone. Next, from the same starting position, try a tight turn halfway around the cone on your backhand. Then, do a tight turn to your forehand to go in the opposite direction and continue right around the far side of the cone toward the net crossing your feet over. Release the puck in motion. Finally, position yourself on the blue line at the boards on your off side, and place the cone on the dot on your proper side. Skate on an angle toward the cone. As you skate through the middle of the ice, take a pass from a player on the blue line at the boards closest to the dot. As you reach the cone, drive around it using cross-overs and shoot in motion at the net. Try moving the cone around, placing it closer to the middle of the ice or up at the top of the circle.

# Skate Moves

Skate moves—playing the puck off your skate and then back to your stick—can be an important part of your deception repertoire. At the same time, it is crucial that you avoid doing a skate move just for the sake of it and only use the skill to accomplish something significant on the ice. Skate moves are risky plays and aren't used often, but they can be very effective in the right situation.

## Vincent Lecavalier Special

**1** Lecavalier's head is up and looking for a potential cross-ice pass. As long as the puck is on the front of his stick blade to the forehand side, Lecavalier is a threat to shoot or pass. Faking the pass buys Lecavalier time and space to execute his off-the-skate move, as any hesitation by a puck carrier can momentarily freeze a defender.

**2** Lecavalier rolls his wrist to bring the heel of his stick off the ice and the toe over the puck.

**3** The puck is behind the heel of his same-side skate and on the toe of his stick blade. When his off-side foot is down flat on the ice, Lecavalier will send the puck between his legs and bank it off his off skate to a position out in front of him.

## The Vincent Lecavalier Special

Like the majority of skate dekes, this move is a pass to yourself that changes the position of the puck and the point of the attack. If executed properly, the Lecavalier Special will allow you to advance forward with the puck while eluding players and protecting the puck from stick checks.

Your goal with the Lecavalier Special is to move the puck through your legs from behind the heel of your same foot, off of your off foot, to a position in front of you on your backhand side. Start with the puck on your forehand side while you are skating toward a defender on your off side. Rotate your upper body far enough so that you are carrying the puck on your forehand behind the heel of your same skate: you should be traveling forward with your feet square to your direction of travel, your shoulders should almost face 90 degrees to your direction of travel on your forehand side and

the puck should be to this side and behind you. Keep your head up.

Almost like the movement of a toe drag, bring the puck in toward the heel of your same skate with the front-side toe of your stick blade. From there, direct the puck between your legs off the inside edge of your off skate, and make sure that your skate blade is facing your direction of travel. You want the puck to deflect off your off skate and continue in front of your off foot. Once the puck is ahead of you, rotate your body to the front, collect the puck and continue driving on your off side.

**Skate Pass to Forehand Drive**

Artturi Lehkonen uses his off foot to kick a loose puck under his leg and to his same side so he can collect it on his forehand as he turns to rush up the ice.

By putting the puck through your legs and off the inside edge of your off skate, you can use your same foot to protect the puck from stick checks coming from your same side. Even if your pass misses your off skate, you are still moving the puck through your legs from behind the heel of your same foot to a position in front of you on your backhand side, which you can skate to—and you are still protecting the puck with your same foot.

## More Skate Moves

### Fake Miss of the Puck

You can also use skate moves and deceptive puck possession to create a gap in defensive coverage, such as by pretending to miss a loose puck in the corner or along the boards with your stick while skating forward, only to move it with the inside edge of your off skate up to your stick as you continue forward. In this instance you are using the "miss" of the puck with your stick to get the defender to hesitate and to momentarily relax the defensive coverage when it appears as though you have missed the puck. Accelerate immediately after you have moved the puck up to your stick to take advantage of the space you have gained through the defender's reaction.

### The Pavel Bure

To quickly change your shooting angle while carrying the puck in a normal puck-carrying position, pass the puck back between your skates to the inside edge of your off foot. Using the inside edge of your off skate, kick the puck past the heel of your same skate and back to your forehand side for a shot. Pavel Bure used this move very effectively to change shooting angles.

The Lecavalier Special is very effective when used on a rush to your off side and combined with a fake shot, especially when the defender commits to blocking the shot, either by "stepping up" or going down in a shot-blocking position. It is also very effective during two-on-ones when you are on your off side. Here, as you move the puck behind to the heel of your same foot, you can fake a cross-ice pass to a teammate on your same side, execute the move and continue to drive around the defender on your backhand side.

### Back Pass Variation

Carrying the puck on your forehand side behind your same skate and rotating your upper body allows you to fake a cross-ice pass to same side. If you keep the puck on your forehand and rotate back a little further while angling your blade back, you can fake a pass to a trailing player. From this position it is easier to complete the Lecavalier Special with a pass off your skate from the back of your stick blade. Once you are rotated and your blade is angled as it would be for a pass to a trailer, lift your blade over the puck so the puck is on the back of your blade, then simply use the back of your blade to send the puck through your legs and off the inside of your off foot.

### Same Skate Variation

Another version of the Lecavalier Special is to pass the puck off the outside edge of your same skate instead of the inside edge of your off skate. When executing this variation you don't need to rotate your shoulders away from your line of travel as much as when doing the standard Lecavalier Special. The deflection off your same skate sends the puck ahead of you on your forehand side, instead of your on backhand side, as it would if the deflection were from your off skate.

Players most often use this variation as a fake before driving to their same side. The same skate variation adds an extra element of deception to the transition between the fake drive to your off side and the actual drive to your same side. With the puck staying on the forehand side, many players like to shoot or pass the puck quickly after this version of the Lecavalier Special, as it changes the angle of the shot or pass.

### One-Handed Backhand Variation

Another variation of the Lecavalier Special starts with the puck on your off side. In this version, the puck is behind you and you are carrying it with one hand on your stick. Pass the puck between your legs and off your same skate (or off the outside edge of your off skate) with the back of your stick blade, and retrieve it in front of you and toward your off side. The difference when using the backhand is that you cannot fake a shot or a pass since you only have one hand on your stick. You are also very vulnerable to checks as your body

is open and turned away from your direction of travel. This backhand version is most effective when you accelerate quickly to your same side, decelerate and rotate your upper body while brining the puck behind you on your off side. Using the backhand skate move, you then direct the puck off your off skate or same skate to a point ahead of you on your off side. You can then accelerate to your off side to retrieve the puck and drive on your off side.

You can also use this variation when you over-skate the puck or when you need to retrieve a pass that is well behind you on your backhand side. If the puck is behind you, reach to your backhand side, direct the puck to your same skate or your off skate and deflect it in front of you to your off side. Bring your stick in front of you and retrieve the puck in one quick movement that allows you to keep your forward momentum. Keep your head up.

### Collecting an Over-Skated Puck

Duncan Keith over-skates the puck and is about to retrieve it with a one-hand backhand pass to himself. Keith keeps his feet moving forward in the direction he is traveling and rotates his upper body to allow his top hand to reach behind him with his stick. A puck in this position can be corralled and sent between the feet (and sometimes off the inside edge of the same skate) to a position where it can be picked up in front of the player. Because Keith is moving forward while looking backward, he is vulnerable to an open ice body-check.

# Lateral Attack Moves

The moves used by elite puck carriers to deke defenders can be quite complicated, sometimes involving double and triple fakes. However, the most effective dekes are often the simplest ones, such as the lateral attack, which involves faking to either your forehand or backhand side, quickly moving the puck across your body to the opposite side, then quickly driving around the defender in this new direction. Lateral attacks are most effective when you accelerate off the fake so the fake is combined with a change of speed to separate yourself from the defender.

### Lateral Attack to the Forehand

A lateral attack to your forehand side allows you to have two hands on your stick at all times and the puck on your forehand after the fake, which is a great advantage because you will have the puck in a shooting or passing position. At its simplest, this move is a fake drive on your backhand side with a quick movement of the puck across your body to your forehand side followed by a drive to your forehand.

The first and most important step is to sell your fake backhand-side drive. Mimic driving to your

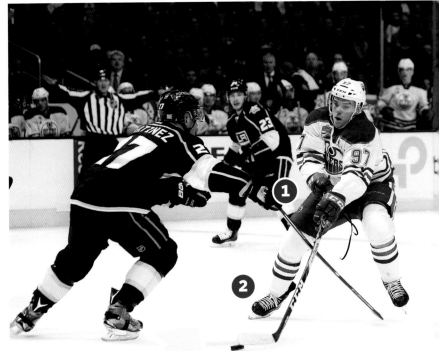

## Fake to the Backhand, Lateral Attack to the Forehand

**①** Connor McDavid's latteral attack to the forehand started with a fake to the backhand, with his hands and arms in the position described in Fig. 66. From here, McDavid has swept the puck across his body, and under the defender's stick, to his forehand side. McDavid's hands are in position to extend his reach as he retrieves the puck on his forehand side.

**②** The backhand fake has frozen the defender for long enough that McDavid's off-side skate is nearly clear of the defender's off skate. McDavid's lateral attack — being made by a drive from the inside edge of his off foot — is so quick that the defender is late to react to the forehand drive.

**③** McDavid thrusts off the inside edge of the heel of his same-side skate in order to drive to open ice (where he has moved the puck) around the late-reacting defender.

**④** McDavid is bending his knee and dropping his shoulder as he leans into the turn around the defenseman. He keeps his off-side skate low to the ice so he can recover quickly from his same-side skate drive. Once he plants his off-side skate, he will be clear of the defender, provided the defenseman's stick doesn't trip him first.

backhand by extending your reach with the puck to your backhand side. When you extend the puck to your backhand side, do so at a 45-degree angle forward, so the puck is still close to you but has also moved closer to the defender (as it would if you were really attacking to your backhand side). Remember that the more you extend the puck away from your body, the further it has to come back and across your body—and the more time and space you need to execute the move. Against players who are focused on playing close to your body it may be better to use a shorter, quicker fake and to extend the puck a shorter distance to your backhand side. The key is to appear to be starting to drive to your backhand side.

Bend your off knee as you extend your reach to your backhand side; this will allow you to drive off your off skate for your forehand attack. When you are ready to execute your forehand attack, bring your same foot underneath you, toward your off foot. Keep your same foot close to the ice. When your same foot meets your off foot, angle your same foot in the direction you want to drive and push off your off foot. Simultaneously bring your hands from your backhand side to your forehand side. Bring your hands across your body, and then push them out, away from your body, to your forehand side by extending your reach. As you move the puck across your body to your forehand side, cup the puck with the back of

**FIG. 66**

### Fake to the Backhand to Lateral Attack to the Forehand

Extend your reach and present the puck to the your backhand side. When you decide to attack to the forehand, bend your knees and bring your same-side foot toward your off-side foot. As you bring the puck toward the middle of your body and push it back out on the forehand side, drive to your forehand side off the inside edge of your off foot; use your same-side foot to lead the drive and then glide. Lead your forehand attack with the puck first and your feet second.

your blade. You may need to draw the puck in toward your body to keep it out of the defender's reach before you push it out to your forehand side with the front of your blade. It is important that you extend the puck to your forehand first and that your body follows.

After your first full stride to your forehand side—driving off your off foot with your same foot leading—continue to accelerate around the defender using cross-overs. Even if you don't need to accelerate after moving to your forehand, such as when you are faking on a goalie, it is still good to bring your same foot underneath you before you drive off the fake as you will have the option to move in any direction when both of your feet are underneath you.

## Lateral Attack to the Backhand

Apply the principles of a lateral attack to your forehand side to a lateral attack to your backhand side, except you need to mirror the attack: for the lateral attack to your backhand you need to fake a forehand drive, move the puck across the defender and drive to your backhand side.

Your fake forehand drive can be short or extended—the more extended the forehand fake, the better you can sell it to the defender, but the longer it takes you to bring the puck back across your body. The forehand fake is usually done with two hands on the

---

# Options off of Lateral Attacks

### Shooting in Motion Through Defenders

Turn defenders into a screen and shoot "through" them after the fake while you're moving off the drive. If the defender turns to cover you on the drive and is able to stay with you, you can release your shot through the defender, as there will be more openings through his or her body or under his or her stick as the defender is no longer square to the puck. With both you and the defender moving when you take the shot, it can become a challenge for the goalie to find the puck through the moving screen. In addition, you are releasing the puck in motion off a fake. Alex Ovechkin does this very effectively.

### Sliding the Puck Across Your Body and Through a Defender

When executing this move you engage defenders so much with your fake drive that they turn to defend the fake, opening up and allowing you to move the

puck through them. The key to this move is to sell the fake drive by accelerating into it. You can use two hands on your stick to your forehand or backhand side, but using one hand and extending your reach to your backhand side might result in the defender "chasing" the puck and being pulled further out of position with the fake. Once the defender has turned to react to the fake drive and is closing in on you, bring the puck, with one or two hands, across your body and through holes in the defender's body (between the feet or through the opening between the defender's stick blade and body). When working your way across the defender's body, depending on how close the check is, you may find you need to draw the puck in toward your body to avoid the puck hitting the defender. Ideally, you will be able to retrieve the puck on the other side of the defender and then drive around the defender.

---

stick, and it is effective when you take a few strides to your forehand to sell the fake. Make sure to bend your same-side knee when extending your reach to your forehand side. This will help you sell the fake, and it will allow you to push off your same leg when you drive to your backhand side.

When you are ready to execute your backhand attack, bring your off foot in toward your same foot and angle it in the direction you want to travel. Keep your off foot close to the ice and drive off your same foot and lead with your off foot. At the same time, bring the puck across your body from your forehand side using the front of your blade while pulling it in toward your body. This will allow you to keep it away from the defender before you push it out to your backhand side with the front of your blade.

You can now drive to your backhand side with the puck on the back of the blade. Extend your reach with the puck by moving it away from your body—and the defender—with one hand (or two hands) on your stick while using cross-overs to accelerate past the defender. The key to this deke, whether using one hand or two, is to move the puck first and then accelerate with cross-overs. If you accelerate during the extension of the puck you will advance on the defender too quickly, allowing the defender to close the gap, giving you less space.

## Lateral Attack with a Heel Turn

During this move you use pressure on the inside edge of the heel of your skate like a brake or rudder to steer you in a different direction.

Unlike the lateral attack to the forehand or backhand, your skates are in a wider stance and stay on the ice. By putting pressure on the inside edge of the heel of one of your skates you will slow yourself down, your momentum will turn your body, and your other foot will turn quickly toward the direction of the skate that is acting like a rudder. Therefore, applying pressure to your right heel will

turn your body to the right, and applying pressure with your left heel will turn you left. To put the most pressure on your heels, lift the front part of your skate off the ice.

Combine a heel turn with the same fakes and puck movements as a lateral attack: fake to the side that you will be turning away from, and bring the puck across your body to the other side, the side that you are turning toward. Remember to bring the puck in toward your body as you bring it across your body to avoid a stick check. The biggest difference between a lateral attack with a heel turn and a traditional lateral attack is that the change of speed that accompanies the change of direction involves deceleration as opposed to acceleration.

A lateral attack with a heel turn is very effective when you need to slow down then quickly change direction on a defender or goalie. A good example would be if you have accelerated toward a defender who has backed into the net and you want to move around the defender quickly to shoot without getting too close to the goalie. Another good opportunity to use a heel turn is when you want to decelerate and move laterally on a breakaway in order to stay out from the goalie and put the puck up high. The move also works extremely well in confined spaces. As with any lateral attack move, when you're in close to a defender or goalie a fake can create openings in a defender that you can move

### Keys to Lateral Attacks

* Sell the fake. Imitate the original movement as closely as possible: use your body and stick placement, as well as your eyes, to sell the fake. Footwork, including aggressive skating into and off the fake, helps as well.
* Quickly bring the puck across your body after the initial fake, before the defender has time to react, and drive in the opposite direction.
* Bring the puck in toward you and away from the defender while moving it across your body. This allows you to avoid stick-on-stick checks by defenders while getting even closer to them when executing attacks, giving them less time to adjust and giving you a more direct line to the net.
* Extend your reach when going around the defender. Extend your arms, bend your knees, bring your hands close together at the top of your stick and rotate your wrists to cup and protect the puck.

the puck through—either as a shot, a pass or a pass to yourself.

When you execute a heel turn in open ice it is very important to use forward cross-overs to drive around your opponent after the heel turn to regain your speed.

# Breakaway Basics

The first rule of any breakaway is that you must "read, react and take." That is, you must read the goalie's position (including the way the goalie adjusts to what you do), react to it and take advantage of what the goalie gives you.

**Speed Is Your Breakaway Ally**

Zach Hyman applies the breaks on Matt Murray, using a change of speed to get Murray to back into his net. Charging forward quickly and slowing down before a shot or deke, as Hyman does here, can move the goalie back into the net, creating more open space to shoot at.

It is important to keep an open mind when attacking a goalie on a breakaway and not decide beforehand what you are going to do, just as when you are deciding how to beat a defender during a rush. You may have a more set plan for a penalty shot or shootout, but even then you have to adapt and react to how the goalie plays you. Generally, if the goalie backs in, leaving more net, you should shoot; if the goalie is out, cutting down the angle and taking away your shot, he or she may be vulnerable to a deke. Speed will play an important factor in your decision making as well. If the goalie is well out from the net but backing up as you approach, you may want to adjust your speed by slowing down to see if the goalie continues to back in, leaving you more net to shoot at. If you are approaching the net with speed, the goalie might not react quickly enough and you may catch the goalie out too far, making it easier to deke. Don't forget that the goalie may do something unexpected in the course of the breakaway or penalty shot, such as sliding out or attempting a poke check. Be willing to improvise. Build up your toolbox of skills and draw from it, keep your options open and just let it happen.

## Be in the Shooting Position

When you get into the "red zone," or scoring area, have the puck in a shooting position even if you might ultimately decide to deke. This way you still have the option to shoot. Mario Lemieux was a master at this. If you are in a scoring position but have the puck in front of you and in the middle of your body, the goalie will sense a deke and react accordingly, as opposed to having to deal with the possibility of both a potential shot or a deke. There are many great dekes that start with the puck in a shooting position or involve a fake shot, giving you many options from this position. More importantly, even if you have decided to deke, the goalie may give you an opening at the last second, and if you are in a shooting position you will still have the option to shoot. Having said that, some players, like Sidney Crosby, are able to move the puck very quickly from a puckhandling position in front of them to a shooting position and release it quickly. However, the general rule is to start with the puck in a

shooting position in order to keep your options open and the goalie guessing.

## Fake Shots Score Big

A convincing fake shot is a great breakaway tool. Even a hesitation with the puck in shooting position can freeze the goalie, allowing you to move to your forehand or backhand side for a quick shot. A fake shot can be as subtle as rotating your top hand to open up your blade (sometimes referred to as a "show and go") or can involve imitating a shooting motion on your forehand or backhand side as illustrated on pages 91 and 92. Usually, once you have faked a shot and moved to your forehand or backhand, you should use an open-bladed shot to get the puck up and over the goalie, who will most likely be low to the ice, moving laterally to shut off the side of the net you are attacking. A fake shot with a quick move to your forehand or backhand (to change your shooting position) along with a quick release to an opening before the goalie can react is also a great move. You can do this move in close or out far, and you can shoot into an open side, up over the goalie or through an opening you created with your lateral attack, such as the five-hole.

## The Same-Foot Fake Is Deadly

A fake shot from your same foot is particularly hard for a goalie to

read because, with one foot raised off the ice, pressure on your stick and your shoulders square to the net, you are a threat to shoot at any time—and you can fake for as long as you can keep your balance since the puck is always in a shooting position. Once you decide to end the fake, you can drop your foot and shoot (off two feet) or move to your forehand or backhand side. Shooting remains an option throughout this fake, even until just before the point at which you move laterally off the fake.

## Hesitation Creates Holes

You can freeze a goalie simply by mimicking a shooting position or quickly opening your blade and moving your top hand away from your body before you make a deke. This hesitation coupled with your hand and blade movement can create holes, as the goalie knows that you may actually shoot the puck using an open-bladed shot in close. Sometimes it will be easier to move the puck through a hole (like the five-hole) that the goalie has provided (by moving laterally) than it will be to maneuver all the way around the goalie.

## Timing Your Release Is Key

Your distance from the net affects when you should release the puck. Goalies can move very well laterally, so gauge when to shoot. Should you shoot for a hole with a quick-release shot immediately after you move the puck laterally to change the shooting angle? Or do you have the room and time to wait until you are around the goalie so you can slip the puck into the open net? Remember, waiting may give the goalie a chance to move laterally and "close the door." It is also important to remember that the more fakes you use, the more time and space you need to execute them. Multiple fakes can be very effective, but you must start them early enough to give yourself the room to execute them. Pressure from checkers on a breakaway may dictate the number of fakes or fake options that are available to you.

## Speed Is Your Breakaway Ally

Changes in speed of any kind create great opportunities to score goals. Charging forward quickly and slowing down before you shoot or deke can move the goalie back into the net, giving you more open space to shoot at. Moving in slowly and then accelerating as you approach the net may allow you to catch the goalie too far out of the net. Of course, on a breakaway your speed options will depend on how close the defenders are and what they are doing. However, on any breakaway, even a partial breakaway, you often have options as far as varying your speed in the red zone. Generally, it is much more effective to move as quickly as you can while maintaining puck control. Moving at a higher speed gives you momentum through any

deke, and it means that the deke can happen quicker, making it harder for the goalie to react and move across to cover the deke or a shot off a fake. It also means that you can slow down as part of your deception, something you can't do if you are already going slowly.

A great way to slow down when in close is to use a heel turn (see page 115). You can steer yourself in the direction you want by putting pressure on the heel of one of your skates. Heel turns are very effective when combined with lateral or vertical attack moves. Jason Spezza and Marian Gaborik are masters at the heel turn.

Players like Alex Kovalev have deceived goalies by changing the anticipated speed of a shot by winding up for a hard shot and then releasing it at half-speed, which is awkward for a goalie to adjust to. However, most openings will only be temporary, and a quick release with a fast shot is most effective.

## Change Your Release Point

This is one of the simplest and most effective moves you can do. By quickly changing where the puck is before you shoot, either by pushing the puck out and away from your body, dragging it in, banking it off your skate or crossing it over your body laterally, you are altering (sometimes only slightly) your shooting angle. If the goaltender does not respond to your puck movement, you will have open spaces to shoot at that weren't

previously there. You can use puck movement when moving straight on the net or when on an angle. It is very effective when you are angling toward the net on your off side and moving the puck toward the center of the net, which will open up the net's far side. Similarly, it is effective when attacking from your proper side, when you can move the puck to the middle of the ice and release it on your backhand toward the far side of the net. The key is to change your shooting point quickly and release the puck quickly, before the goalkeeper has time to adjust.

## Change Your Approach to the Net

Many players have had success on shootouts or penalty shots by approaching the net from an angle or on a curved approach, in particular by moving from their off side toward the middle of the ice. Sometimes players do this to set up a particular deke, like coming in on an angle from the off side to execute the Forsberg one-handed extension (see page 120) or the spinorama/tight turn move (see page 122) in close. At other times, players want to present a moving approach to see if the goalie makes a positioning mistake when adjusting to their approach, leaving an opening that the player can take advantage of.

## Get the Puck Up Quickly

It is very important to be able to get the puck up quickly when you

**Same-Foot Heel Turn**
David Krejci uses speed and a lightning-quick heel turn from his same foot in order to deke forehand to backhand. Because Krejci executed the move quickly and close to the net, the goalie can't move backward laterally to his blocker-side post in time to make the save. Krejci is left with a mostly open net, and the goalie's only option will be to swat at Krejci with his stick while driving backward with his upper body to try and cover the open net.

are in close. Goalies are becoming better and better at moving laterally and taking away the low part of the net. However, a quick lateral move off a fake with a quick shot into the top part of the net is very difficult for any goalie to stop. The open-bladed shot is great to get the puck up quickly off your forehand or backhand side. Some coaches call this shot a "3–11," meaning 3 feet, 11 inches—or just under the crossbar, which is 4 feet off the ice. Other coaches will ask their players to aim for the water bottle that invariably sits on top of the goalie's net. Either way the message is clear: when in close, get the puck up.

## Double Dekes Can Beat Great Goalies

Double dekes are an excellent way to beat a goalie who has great anticipation and great lateral movement. The key to double faking is to start your move far enough away from the net that you still have room to get the puck up off your second deke if necessary. A very effective double fake involves a fake shot (forehand or backhand) followed by a lateral deke while moving to the opposite side before quickly returning to the side you originally faked from. Couple your fakes with the foot movements used when attacking laterally so you can accelerate when shifting direction, or, alternatively, use heel turns (above) or outside-edge reverses (see page 126) so you can slow down to give yourself more space to get the puck up.

# The Forsberg

Perhaps the ultimate move used to change the position of the puck and the angle to the net is when players use one hand on their stick to extend their reach and change the position of the puck, the way Peter Forsberg famously did to defeat Canada and clinch gold for Sweden at the 1994 Lillehammer Olympics.

## Forsberg Finish

**1** Anze Kopitar's hand is at the top of his stick, and he has extended his reach as far as he can to his backhand side to sweep the puck into the open net.

**2** Kopitar's fake to the far side (the goalie's stick side) is so successful that he nearly runs into the goalie (who bit hard on the fake) before he completes the move. This causes Kopitar to lose his balance. Ideally, Kopitar would bend his off-side knee and evenly distribute his weight over his off-side skate, which would be on a flat blade. This would allow Kopitar to be in a position to raise the puck on his backhand with a one-handed shot.

## Method

You can attack the net straight on with this move, but it is much better to come in from an angle on your off wing, as the move relies heavily on lateral movement to create an opening for the puck. Start by attacking the net from your off side with the puck on your forehand side, and then drift into the middle of the ice so the puck is in the middle of the ice and your momentum is moving you from the near post to the far post. Once in the middle, fake a shot to the far side of the net, freezing the goalie momentarily. Remember to sell the fake with your body, stick and, most importantly, your eyes.

As you fake, move across the net to the far side as if to deke to your forehand side, but start to move the puck to your backhand, against the flow of your movement, and ultimately extend your reach all the way to your backhand with only one hand on your stick. Your body, and most likely the goalie, will end up near the far post, while your reach will enable you to extend your arm across the crease for a tap into the open part of the net.

Against very skilled goalies, who might anticipate this move, you can fake a shot to the far post and then extend your reach with the puck to your forehand side before moving the puck against the flow to your backhand side. This extra

puckhandling will force the goalie to track the puck to the far post, leaving the near side of the net wide open. If your fake shot is good enough to freeze the goalie, it may cause the goalkeeper to make a desperate attempt to stay with you as you advance on the forehand to the far post, leaving you with even more net on the near side.

Be mindful of a poke check as you bring the puck from your forehand to your backhand. And to avoid being stopped by a goalie's stick on a desperate lunge to cover the open net, try to raise the puck on your one-handed backhand shot.

### The Original

Peter Forsberg eludes Corey Hirsch with his now famous move. Forsberg started his move with speed and on an angle from his off side (Hirsch's glove side; the near side of the net). After dekeing to the far side of the net (Hirsch's blocker side), Forsberg's speed carried him further to the far side, where he simultaneously extended his reach with the puck to his backhand and executed a heel-to-heel turn, which allowed him to face into the turn and extend his reach as far as possible.

# The Spinorama

 This move is also known as the Savardian Spinorama, named after NHL greats Serge Savard and Denis Savard. Both players used the move as a deke around opposing players to get to open ice or to the goal, but it was seldom used directly on goalies.

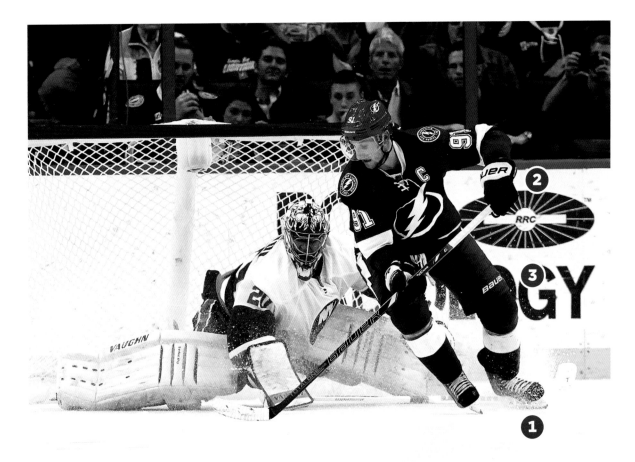

## Spinorama Backhand Release

**1** Steven Stamkos, a right-handed shot, executes a tight turn to the backhand — using the outside edge of his same foot and the inside edge of his off foot — to finish his spinorama. His turn originated off of a drive to the goalie's blocker side.

**2** Stamkos holds his top hand up and away from his body to keep his stick blade square to the ice throughout the spinorama. He rotates his wrist slightly to close his stick blade over the puck for control — this also allows him to be in the proper shooting position for a backhand shot when he exits the spinorama.

**3** With the goalie conceding the entire top half of the net, Stamkos will bend his knees as he completes the spinorama and lower his hands to allow him to elevate his backhand shot over the goalie's pad.

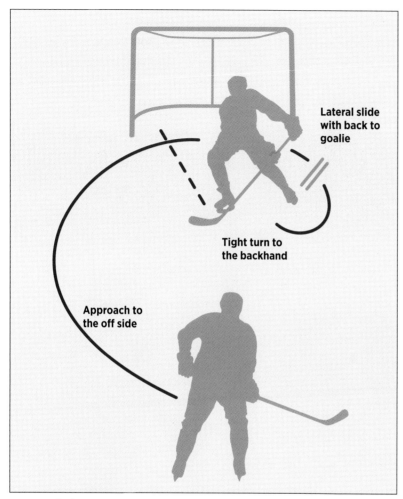

Lateral slide
with back to
goalie

Tight turn to
the backhand

Approach to
the off side

**FIG. 67 Spinorama**

## Method

A Spinorama is best when executed with speed coming from an angle on your off side. Attack the net with the puck on your forehand side and skate hard toward the far side post, selling the shot to the far side the entire way. As you get right in on the goal, you should be closer to the far side than to the near side, put the puck on your backhand side and initiate a lateral slide with your rear toward the net.

From your lateral slide you need to execute a tight turn to your backhand side, bringing the puck away from the goalie and back to the near side of the net. The goalie should be down and out, having moved with you laterally toward the far side of the net, leaving the near side open for you to slip the puck into the net on your backhand as you come out of your tight turn.

# The Datsyuk

As dekes become more popular and the shootout continues to be an important part of NHL action, players have begun to introduce new and innovative moves to their list of possible ways to beat goalies. Pavel Datsyuk's signature vertical and lateral move is a great example of a how a skilled player can combine existing elements to create something new and effective.

## Method

It's best to start this move as a straightaway attack with speed. As you reach the hash marks in the slot, pull the puck back on your forehand side and fake a same-foot shot to the near side of the net (stick side for left-handed players, trapper side for right-handed players). Raise your off foot from the ice during the same-foot fake shot to help sell the fake, and push the puck forward as though you are going to release it toward the near side of the net. When you reach the release point of the shot, don't pull the trigger; instead, push your top hand away from your body, lift your stick over the puck and drag the puck toward you with the back of your blade. At the same time, pivot your same skate so the toe angles toward your off side, and glide on this angled skate across the front of the net, toward the far side and away from your fake. This should move you away from the goalie and toward the open net on the far side, as the goalie will be recovering from your

## Angling Away from the Goalie

**1** Pavel Datsyuk started his move with a straightaway attack and a fake same-foot shot to the near side (Harding's glove side).

**2** Datsyuk is currently in the middle of his move, angling his same foot toward his off side, sending him away from Harding and toward the far side of the net.

**3** His off foot is returning to the ice from its elevated position during the same-foot fake. This will help him to glide.

**4** He lifts the blade of his stick over the puck so he can handle it on his backhand. Datsyuk will then continue to glide toward his off side (the far side of the net), dragging the puck with him on his backhand, until he is clear of Harding, at which point Datsyuk will put the puck on his forehand and raise it into the net.

---

### Practicing the Datsyuk Drag

Assume the hockey-playing position. Place a glove on the ice two to three feet in front of your same skate and place a puck on the ice between your skate and your glove. With your skates stationary, handle the puck around the glove. First, move the puck with the front of your blade around the outside of the glove. When you get to the top of the glove, push your top hand away from your body and lift your blade over the puck. Now drag the puck on the backside of your blade around the top and the inside of the glove, until you reach your original position. Repeat.

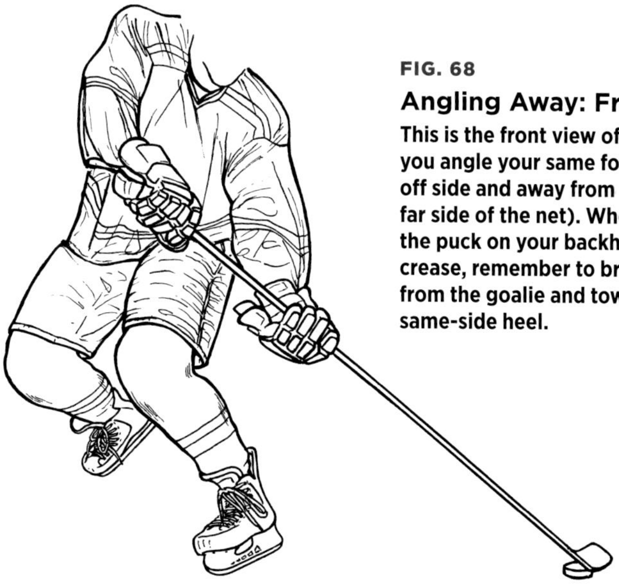

**FIG. 68**

**Angling Away: Front View**
This is the front view of the Datsyuk as you angle your same foot toward your off side and away from the goalie (the far side of the net). When you drag the puck on your backhand across the crease, remember to bring it away from the goalie and toward your same-side heel.

---

fake to the near side.

To avoid a poke check and to get around the goalie while moving to the far side, drag the puck slightly behind your same heel—your body from the torso up will be rotated much the same way that it is during the Lecavalier Special (see page 108). As you begin to move further to the far side, you can bring your off foot down, creating a weight transfer, which will help you glide to the far side. When clear of the goalie (at which point you will be almost beside the far-side post), lift your stick over the puck to place the puck on the front of your blade and shoot it into the net on your forehand. By the time you have the puck on your forehand and have worked your way across the goalmouth, the goaltender should be down and out on the other side of the net, leaving you with a wide-open cage. However, beware of a last-ditch dive across the net from the goalie—get that puck up.

# Outside-Edge Reverse

This move will allow you to deke a goalie with a quick and drastic change of direction. It is effective when used approaching the net from the proper side as a single fake, but also as part of a larger triple fake!

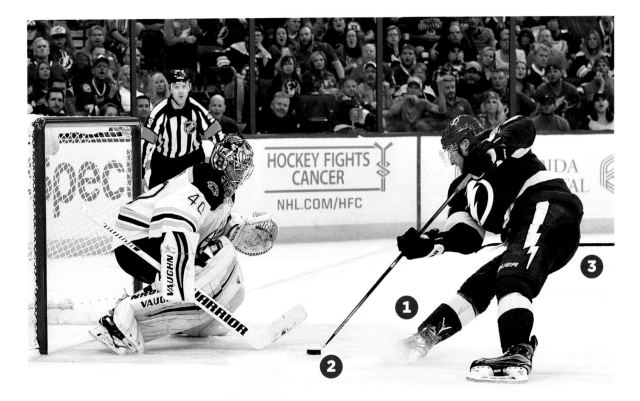

## Reverse to the Forehand

**1** Steven Stamkos drives the outside edge of his same foot into the ice ahead of him. By doing so, he radically alters his direction of travel, from a drive on his backhand to the far side of the net (the goalie's stick side) to a deke across the face of the net to his forehand side.

**2** Stamkos is going to carry the puck on his backhand to deke across the face of the net to his forehand side. With his top hand raised up, he will pull the puck in toward his body with his bottom hand in order to protect the puck from a stick check by the goalie. As he moves across the net in front of the goalie, he will bring the puck to his

forehand and bring his top hand up and into his body in order to be able to lift the puck over the goalie and into the top of the net.

**3** In order to push the goalie back into the net as far as possible, Stamkos has executed his outside-edge reverse very close to the net. By leaning back, his reverse will take him away from the goalie. The further Stamkos moves away from the net, the more net there will be for him to shoot at when he arrives with the puck on his forehand on the other side of the net. Stamkos' lean will also enable him to get the puck up high quickly.

## Method

Ultimately this move comes down to quickly reversing your direction of travel (from side to side) by using the outside edge of your skate blade on your same foot. To do this, as you are skating toward your off side and all of your weight is on your off foot, plant the outside edge of your same foot perpendicular to your direction of travel—your heel will point to your off side and your toe will point to your proper side. By planting the outside-edge of your skate hard into the ice and by bending your knee, you will absorb the energy from your stride and move your body in the reverse direction of the way you were traveling. The more you bend your same leg, the closer to your body the blade contacts the ice and the quicker the reverse is initiated. The harder you drive the blade into the ice, the quicker the acceleration off the reverse. As soon as the reverse is initiated, the off foot follows the path of the lead foot, also carving on the outside edge.

## The Ultimate Triple Deke

Set up the deke by carrying the puck in position to shoot a forehand shot from your proper side. Either hesitate with the puck in that position or fake a shot by bringing your top hand toward your body and opening up your blade. This will hold the goalie enough so that they will have to scramble to follow you on your next move. The fake following the first move is a hard drive to your off side. Move the puck from forehand to backhand and use a couple of quick cross-over steps to sell this fake. This will set you up for what looks like a backhand shot toward the off side as you move across the front of the net from your proper side to your off side. Now it is time for the outside-edge reverse. In the middle of your cross-over drive to your off side, take your same foot as it is raised off the ice pointing toward the off side—your weight is entirely on your off foot—and quickly reverse your same foot in the air so that your heel points toward your off side and your toe points toward your proper side. Then extend the leg of your same foot to bring the outside edge of the blade on your same foot skate into contact with the ice in front of you at 90 degrees to your direction of travel. As you move toward your proper side, you can lean back and extend your legs, to reduce the weight and resistance on your blades, increasing your speed, and you can bring your hands in toward your body and open up your blade to give you the option to raise the puck high if necessary.

## Tip

With both feet pointing straight ahead shoulder width apart and stationary on the ice, lift up your same foot and move it in front of you in the "reverse" position with the heel pointing toward your off side and the toe pointing toward your proper side. Bring the outside edge of the blade into contact with the ice at 90 degrees to the direction you are facing. Initially just scrape a layer off the ice using your outside edge. Try this both with a straight leg and a bent leg. Next, take a stride with your same foot before trying the same movement, this time, as opposed to just scraping the ice, carve a little on the outside edge toward your proper side. As you gain confidence, add more and more speed into the reverse and eventually add a couple of cross-over steps. Once you can execute all of the steps together, add a puck and practice executing the move with control and then speed. Ultimately you will develop a drastic but seamless outside-edge reverse, which you can use as the crucial part of a great deke!

# Face-Off Techniques

Puck possession is crucial to offensive success, and every face-off presents an opportunity to gain possession of the puck. Face-offs are particularly important during special teams play and in the offensive and defensive zones.

### Reverse Bottom-Hand Grip

In this face-off, both forwards elect to use the reverse bottom-hand grip in an attempt to win the puck back to their teammates. Both players have their bottom hands low on the shaft for leverage, but the timing, eye-hand coordination and inside blade placement of Ryan Nugent-Hopkins has him at an advantage to win this face-off. Note the players in the foreground have already started to move toward the face-off dot to help try to win the draw.

### Entering a Draw

Some face-off approaches increase your chances of winning the draw. Before you get ready for the face-off, take a quick moment to make sure all of your teammates are in proper position. This not only means they are in position to defend, but also in position to get to a loose puck off the face-off. Many teams win draws by having the first player to a loose puck off

the face-off. Remember, many face-offs are not won clean, and the puck is loose close to the dot after the draw. In a face-off, note which hand your opposing center is and try to predict what he or she will likely do on the draw, taking the face-off location into account.

When you are ready, start to move into a legal position to take the draw. Your feet should be wide enough apart to give you balance and a good support base, but not so wide that you can't move quickly off the draw to grab a loose puck. Bend your knees so you are in a solid hockey-playing position, since there is often contact off the draw, but don't bend them so deep that it restricts your ability to get to a loose puck quickly.

You should choke up on your stick, moving your top hand down the shaft and your bottom hand toward the blade. This will bring you fairly low to the ice. You should lean forward so that your upper body is close to the dot. The blade of your stick should be low and close to the ice, but don't initially put all of your weight on your stick, as this will hinder you from being quick with your stick on the draw. A quick stick is crucial to face-off success. Your weight should be on the balls of your feet, to give you balance and strength on your skates and so you can drive off quickly to move to a loose puck, especially if you are going to move forward quickly off the drop of the puck or try to "spin" into your opponent.

Just before the draw, look again at the opposing center. Look for anything in the positioning of your opponents' stick or body that will tip you off about their intentions. Decide if you can use their position to your advantage. For example, if your opposition is drawing the puck back to one side and you want to move the puck forward to the same side, perhaps to clear the

**The Sweep**
Jonathan Toews (No. 19) will likely win this face-off against Teuvo Teravainen (No. 86). Toews has lined up for the draw using a forehand grip and has swept his blade to the backhand against his opponent's stick. He will follow with a sweep to the forehand to win the puck to the "closed" side of the dot (where the linesman is standing). Both players have choked up on their sticks for added strength and quicker reaction time.

zone, you can use your opponent's draw motion to move the puck closer to your targeted area.

Before the drop, decide how you want to win the draw and exactly what you are going to do to succeed. It is generally easier to draw the puck toward the linesman or referee, since you can angle your body and stick into the "open" side of the dot (opposite where the linesman is standing) and still be in a legal position. This will give you an advantage if you draw toward the linesman. This is why, for example, on a draw in the defensive zone to their goalie's right, left-hand centers may wish to draw the puck on their forehand into the corner even though they are stronger when drawing on their backhand, since the linesman is always on the board side of the dot.

When you are in the proper position before the drop, with your feet in the proper position and your stick at the bottom of the dot, focus on the puck in the linesman's hand. Be ready to explode quickly with your hands and arms off the drop of the puck. Lean forward as far as possible into the face-off dot while keeping your feet in the proper and legal position for the draw. The closer your upper body is to your stick's point of impact with the puck, the better you can use your body weight to give you strength on the draw. Be ready to use your feet to move a loose puck off the draw to a teammate.

**The Spin**
Jaden Schwartz uses a spin move off the face-off to put himself between his face-off opponent and the puck, likely ensuring a clean win back to his defense pairing. Schwartz's spin has also blocked the stick of his opponent so that even if he does lose the puck battle, his opponent can't move the puck backward as he originally planned. Lastly, Schwartz's spin opens up the dot for his teammates to come help grab a loose puck.

## Faceoff Techniques

### The Reverse Bottom-Hand Grip

Reversing your bottom-hand grip will give you a very strong "pull" back on your backhand to your forehand side or through your legs. The disadvantages of this grip include that the opposing center will likely know where you intend to draw the puck and, if you don't win the draw clean, you will probably have to quickly change your grip to battle for or handle a loose puck off the draw. In the offensive zone, keep in mind that you may get an opportunity to shoot or pass a loose puck from near the face-off dot after a draw. Holding your stick normally may allow you to take advantage of an opportunity to score right off the face-off. With a reverse bottom-hand grip, it is also difficult to adjust or to change your approach mid-draw or just before the draw. Despite these disadvantages, many players like the reverse grip since it gives them added strength on the draw on their backhand, which is especially important if you and the opposing center contact the puck at the same time.

### Choking Up on the Top-Hand Grip

This technique has many advantages. It can help give you a quicker and more accurate path to the puck, like a baseball player choking up on the bat. If there is a puck battle in the face-off circle off the draw, this grip gives you added strength on your stick. It is especially effective when combined with a reverse bottom-hand grip, providing a strong "pull" on your backhand to your forehand side. The disadvantage is that you may have to adjust your top-hand grip when you battle for or handle a loose puck off the draw or when you move to defense off the draw.

## Fake Change

If you are skilled at drawing on your backhand with a normal grip and with a reverse grip, try showing your opponent a reverse grip and then turning your grip to a normal grip just before the draw. Your opponent will think you intend to draw on your forehand or to move forward to tie up the opposing center. Then, on the puck drop, draw on your backhand. The other center may not be ready for a quick draw on your backhand, giving you the opportunity to win a clean face-off.

## The Sweep

The sweep refers to sweeping the blade of your stick on the ice in a semicircular motion, either on your forehand or backhand, and then sweeping the puck. This technique is effective, since sweeping your stick on the ice gives your shot extra strength. Even if your opponent's stick gets to the puck first, if you have a strong sweeping motion, you can still win the draw. You can sweep with either a normal grip or a reverse grip.

## Drop and Chop or Drop and Pop

This technique involves moving your stick in the air forward, past the puck, and then dropping it down to contact the puck and "chop" or "pop" it on your forehand or backhand. This is a useful technique for players who have a great stick and good timing and can contact the puck just as it contacts the ice. You can drop and chop with a normal grip or a reverse grip, but players usually execute this technique much quicker with a normal grip.

## Forward Tap and Draw Back

In this technique, you hold your stick normally and quickly move the blade forward as the puck is being dropped, "tapping" the opposing player's stick on the blade or the shaft just above the blade in a forward motion before sliding your blade back to contact the puck and draw it back. The "tap" is really a strike, quick but strong. This technique is most effective when facing off against a player who shoots the same way you do. You must be aware of the location of the other player's stick at all times. Timing is always important in a face-off, but it is crucial when using this technique. If you move too early for the initial "tap," you will be waived out of the circle. If you are too late, you could knock the puck ahead when you don't intend to. Time it right, and you will have a clean draw unhindered by the opposing player. It can produce a great scoring chance in the offensive zone.

## Tie Up and Kick

In this technique you move forward quickly off the draw, briefly tie up your opponent's stick and then use your feet to kick the puck back to one of your teammates. You can tie up your opponent's stick by simply sweeping your stick forward so that its shaft contacts the shaft of your opponent's stick just above the blade. If your stick is on the ice and its shaft is against your opponent's shaft, it will be very difficult for your opponent to move that stick. You don't have to tie up your opponent's stick for very long to get your feet on the puck and kick it back.

A variation of this technique is the spin and kick, in which you lead with your stick against your opponent's stick and spin your body to turn into the opposing player so that you are between the opposing center and the puck, allowing you to move the puck with your skate. Again, timing and quickness are crucial. Jump too early and you will be waived out of the circle. Move too late and your opponent will have already drawn the puck back. If that happens, you are at least in a good defensive position in relation to the opposing center. Hopefully your efforts to tie up the opposing center's stick will have prevented a clean draw and one of your teammates can quickly move to cover the player receiving the draw or jump on the loose puck.

# Tip-Ins

With the prevalence of "net front pressure," more goals than ever before are being scored off tip-ins and deflections. To take advantage of a screened goalkeeper and the heavy traffic in front of the net, it is sometimes wiser not to shoot to score—often, very little net is visible to the shooter—but to instead shoot at your teammates for tip-ins.

## Screen, Tip and Spin

**1** Tom Pyatt is holding his stick in the hockey-playing position and pointing its toe in the direction of the shooter.

**2** Pyatt is as close to the top of the crease and to the goalie as possible without making contact with the goalkeeper. He has positioned himself perfectly to take away the goaltender's line of sight of the shot.

**3** Pyatt has tipped the puck and has immediately turned his head and shoulders to track the puck. If the puck is saved and a rebound is available, it will be Pyatt's job to get to the rebound first.

## Set Up

When your team gets puck possession in the offensive zone and moves it to the point or high slot, ideally a teammate should be in the middle slot area, between the hash marks. Here, the mid-slot player can deflect a puck shot from the point. The mid-slot player will usually be moving through the mid-slot during the shot and not stationary. The mid-slot player can be on an angle to the shooter, with his or her stick in or near the shooting lane. A second teammate should be stationary, directly in front of the goaltender and facing the shooter. This teammate's approach is to screen, tip and rebound.

## Tipping and Reaction

When executing the screen, tip and rebound, make sure you are between the puck and the goalie prior to the shot, with your back to the goalie, your skates just outside of the blue paint and your knees bent in a solid stance. You should thereby be an effective screen for the shot. To tip the shot, the blade of your stick should be toward the shooter. When the shot is taken, you can tip the puck, ideally with the blade of your stick but also with the shaft, through or to the side of your body. The goal is to change the direction of the puck with very little change to the speed of the shot. Therefore, keeping the blade of your stick pointed toward the shooter and angling it slightly to tip the puck is superior to tipping a shot from a blade that is square to the shooter.

When you tip the puck, spin to face the goalie and look for a rebound. If the goaltender deflects the puck or the rebound goes into the corner or into the side of the net, you must be the first player on the loose puck so that your team can keep possession. In the words of Mike Babcock, the player in front of the net must "control the front of the net, the back wall and the offensive corners." To be most effective, you must have quick hands, good hand-eye coordination, the athletic ability to get into a good position and get to rebounds, the courage and character to stand in front of the net, and the speed to be the first from the front of the net to the end boards or corners to successfully chase down and battle for any loose pucks. Awareness of how the play is developing in the offensive zone and the timing needed to move into position to screen at the right moment are also important factors to be effective when creating net front pressure. Once you've mastered this skill you will be a great offensive weapon!

## Drill

Even young players can learn the skill of deflecting a puck toward the net while facing the shooter.

Five players place themselves stationary around a circle, all facing the dot, and you take position on the dot. Start with one of the players on the circle with a puck and face this player. The player with the puck then passes the puck in between your feet, and you point the blade of your stick toward the shooter and try to deflect the puck through your legs to a player who is behind you and stationed on the circle. Players can pass the puck harder and harder as you learn the skill. Spin to follow the deflected puck and face the player who is receiving the deflected puck, and that player then passes the puck in between your feet. Increase the pace as your skill increases, and then add a second puck to really keep everyone moving.

Older players can run this drill in the middle circle with the players positioned back from the circle and execute harder and harder passes. As you master the skill, try some passes off the ice. You will learn to point the toe of your stick blade toward the passer and angle the blade to use the middle and heal of the blade to direct the puck without slowing down the pass or shot much. Once you've acquired this skill, move to in front of the net, with or without a goalie, and try tipping shots from the point. Remember to spin to follow the deflected shot so that you always screen, tip and rebound.

# 4 Drills

Buffalo Sabres prospects change direction with tight turns in a drill at the Sabres' development camp in the summer of 2017.

# Inside-Out Weave

## Purpose

Teaches and imprints many physical skills, including skating with speed, both frontward and backward, while negotiating turns and transitions with proper edge-work while skating with a puck or looking to receive a pass or to make a pass. Also teaches mental skills, including anticipation, vision and the ability to read and react, among others.

## Setup

You can set up the drill as a full-ice, half-ice or cross-ice drill (in the offensive zone). Players on the course act as moving pylons/obstacles for the other players. There should be 10–12 players moving on the full ice, and all players must keep their heads up at all times. Levels 2 and 4 are illustrated.

## Legend

↗ Forward skating

↗ Backward skating

↗ Pass or shot

**F** Forward player

**D** Defensive player

**C** Coach

X○ Players

## Drill

**Level 1:** Players handle the puck through the course. The line starts at the dot. The next player leaves when the player in front goes around the first cone. Players make tight turns around the cones then cross-overs to accelerate to the next cone and to the net.

**Level 2:** The player goes forward through the course without the puck. The coach is on the side of the net opposite to the start of the line and passes a puck to the player as soon as he or she goes around last cone. To receive the pass, the player has to get open.

**Level 3:** Same as level 2, but players skate backward through the course to the last cone and then turn at the last cone to skate forward and look for a pass from the coach.

**Level 4:** Same as level 2, but players skate forward to the first cone, backward to the next cone and continue until skating forward after the last cone to receive a pass from the coach.

**Levels 5 and 6:** Players skate backward through the course with the puck and then skate forward to the first cone and backward to the next cone and continue, always with the puck.

**Level 7:** Start with a player at each cone. The player at the dot passes to the player at the first cone, who passes to the player at the next cone until the puck reaches the player at the last cone, who receives the pass and attacks the net. Each player follows their pass immediately after making it.

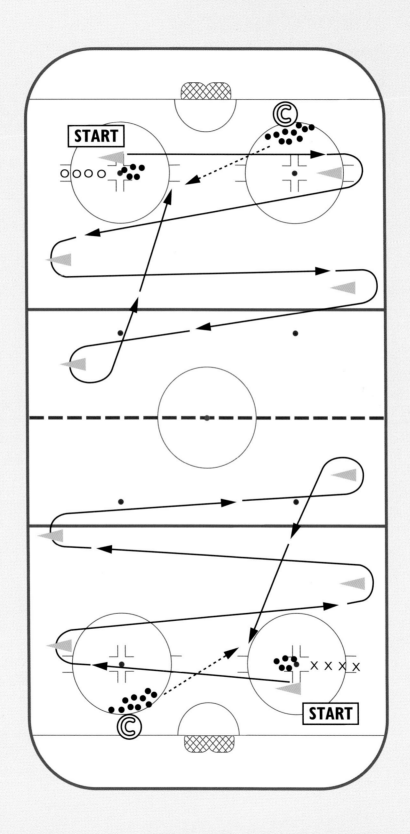

# Wild Walkover Course

## Purpose

This is the best drill to teach the proper method of crossing over and crossing under (with ankle extensions), as well as how to skate with a puck through traffic. Trains players to keep their head up so as to avoid contact with other players on the course.

## Setup

Drill is set up either along one side or both sides of the ice, with players at both ends and pucks at one end. Players doing walkovers on the course act as moving pylons for the players with pucks. There can be up to 20 players moving on the course at one time.

## Drill

Players starting in the end without pucks skate from the hash marks to the blue line. At the blue line, the players execute lateral walkovers (the first step to learning cross-overs, cross-unders and lateral movement).

Players cross skates (outside skate over inside skate as dictated by the direction of travel) and end each cross-over by planting their entire blade flat on the ice — players should not "run" on the toes of their blades. Ankles should be relaxed, and the ankle of the skate crossing under should rotate to keep the blade on ice as the other leg crosses over.

The stick of a player doing walkovers should always be between their shoulders, and their shoulders should be square, 90 degrees to the direction of travel. More skilled players can carry a puck on walkovers.

Walkover players skate hard between the lines and finish the walkover portion of the course with forward cross-overs on the far circle before joining the line of players with pucks.

Players starting in the end with pucks practice moves on players walking over as if they are defenders. Players carrying a puck finish with a shot on net.

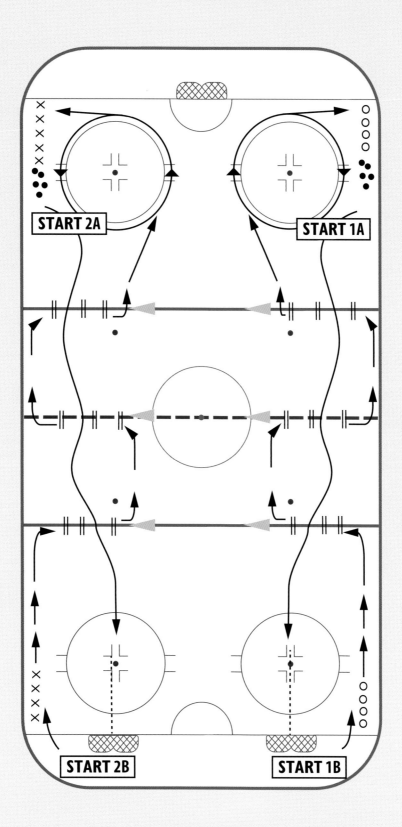

START 2A

START 1A

START 2B

START 1B

# Wow Drill

## Purpose

To practice skating with speed, both frontward and backward, while negotiating tight turns and transitions with proper edge-work while skating with a puck or looking to receive a pass. Also trains players to keep their head up in order to avoid contact with other players on the course and to negotiate a 1-on-1 net drive.

## Setup

Drill is set as a full-ice exercise (backward-forward variant shown). Players start in two groups. Players on the course act as moving pylons/obstacles for the other players. Defenders in the crease should rotate into the drill so they too complete the course. Level 2 is illustrated. The drill was named "Wow" because, from the air, it shows as two Ws with an O (the center ice circle) in the middle.

## Drill

**Level 1:** Carry the puck forward through entire course. Players leave when the player in front goes around the first cone.

**Level 2:** No puck through the course. Start from the hash marks, skating backward to the first cone, forward to the next cone, backward to the next cone, and forwards to receive a pass from the coach at the closest face-off dot at the blue line.

**Level 3:** Same as level 1. Add a defender in the crease who advances, tracks a player on the course to the last cone and plays the player 1-on-1 to the net. Players alternate between playing defense and being on the course.

**Level 4:** Same as level 2 but add a defender as in level 3.

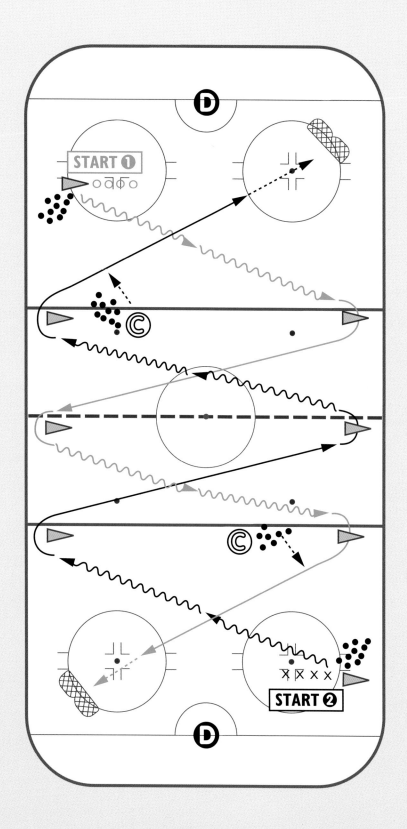

# Cyclone

## Purpose

To practice skating with speed while carrying a puck through traffic, with emphasis on controlling the puck through tight turns and around obstacles. Also teaches mental skills, including anticipation, vision and the ability to read and react.

## Setup

Drill is set up as a full-ice exercise with four shooting stations (players take two shots per cycle). Players start in two groups at the beginning of the wow drill course (near the gates). Players on the course act as moving pylons/obstacles for the other players. Keep your head up!

## Drill

Similar to the wow drill, but with an added full-ice weave attack.

Players carry the puck forward through the wow drill and fire the puck on net. After firing on net, the player picks up a new puck (near the gate) and attacks the far net. The player must weave with the puck to the other end of the ice, through all of the players completing the wow drill, to attack the net at the far end before rejoining the line at the gate where they first started. All players keep their heads up at all times!

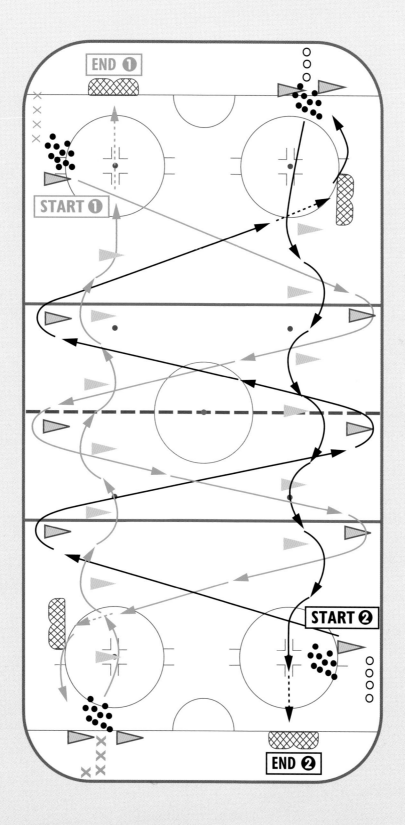

# Vortex

## Purpose

To teach the proper method of crossing over and crossing under (using ankle extensions), as well as how to skate in proper position (with or without a puck) while turning. Trains players to keep their head up in order to avoid contact with other players on the course.

## Setup

The drill is set up with two half-ice circuits converging at center ice. Players start from opposite hash marks and end in the same end in which they started. Level 4 (forward skating with puck) is illustrated. Tip: Put one coach in the center circle, skate the circle in the direction the players should be traveling to help keep everyone focused.

## Drill

**Level 1:** Without a puck, players skate forward around the circles, emphasizing body and stick position to maximize glide, acceleration and speed on cross-overs. Stick blade should always be on the circle, with the top hand across the body and underneath the bottom hand forearm. After exiting the center-ice circle, players pick up a puck for a drive and shot on net.

**Level 2:** Without a puck, players skate backward around the circles, emphasizing body and stick position to maximize glide, acceleration and speed on cross-overs. Stick blade should always be on the circle, with the top hand away from the body to keep the stick blade square to the ice. After exiting the center-ice circle, players turn forward and pick up a puck for a drive and shot on net.

**Level 3:** Combine the first two levels, with transitions from forward to backward at every hash mark.

**Level 4, 5 and 6:** Same as Levels 1, 2 and 3, but carrying a puck through the course. In these levels the coach acts as checker at the red line.

# Spiral

## Purpose

For the player moving through the course, the drill teaches heads-up skating, passing and puck protection (all executed with speed). For the players in the other positions, emphasis is on timing, passing, quick puck movement and accuracy. The players competing at the end of the drill get to practice 1-on-1 tactics.

## Setup

Drill is set up either along one side or both sides of the ice. For each course there are five positions:

**1** Skater through course

**2** Puck passer

**3** Puck passer

**4** Puck passer

**5** Defender on rush

Players start at position 1 and rotate through all positions. For a lighter variation of the drill, eliminate the defender guarding the net drive.

## Drill

**Level 1:** Player at position 1 leaves the hash marks without a puck, takes a pass from the player in position 2 and skates forward to execute a tight turn around a cone before executing a give-and-go pass with the player in position 3. The player from position 1 repeats the same maneuver at the next cone, executing a give-and-go with the player in position 4. The player from position 1 then attacks the goalie at the far end while the player from position 5 defends against the net drive. The player from position 1 then moves to position 5 and rotates through all positions to end up back at position 1. Players start after the player in front of them has executed the first give-and-go pass.

**Level 2:** Players on the course execute a "double transition" around each cone. This skating maneuver starts with a forward slide into a forward-to-backward transition around the cone and then a backward-to-forward transition to accelerate away from the cone before taking the pass. This is one of the best maneuvers to teach players seamless transitions; transferring momentum through the transition and into backward and forward power starts.

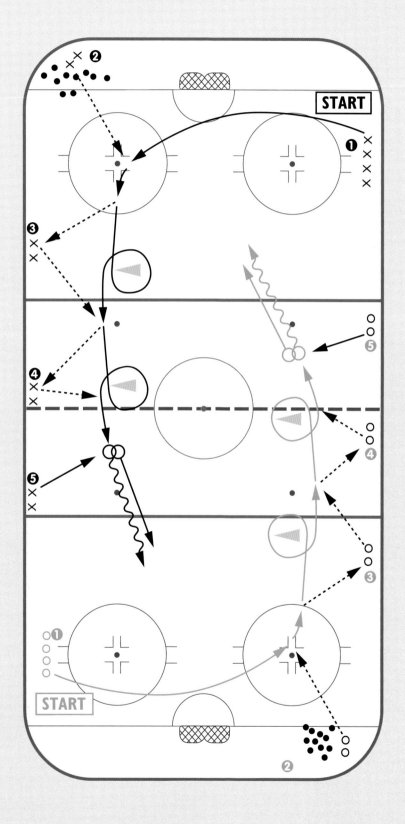

# D on the Dots

## Purpose

To teach lateral mobility, quick puck movement and a good first pass by your defender.

## Setup

Coach is in the middle with a puck and two defensive pairings on the face-off dots.

## Drill

The coach passes the puck from the center dot to one of the four defenders, who are moving back and forth and up and back between the dot and the red line. The coach then "forechecks" the defenders, who must move laterally before passing the puck to one of the other defenders in the drill. Rotate in a third defensive pair every 30–40 seconds.

# 2-on-2 Down Low

## Purpose

To teach forwards offensive zone possession and scoring skills; to teach defenders defensive skills and how to apply pressure in a confined space.

## Setup

Two forwards are on the hash marks facing the goal line; two defenders are on either side of the dot facing the blue line. Coach is in the middle with the puck.

## Drill

On the coach's signal, the defenders skate forward about 6 feet (2 m) above the circle and then backward towards the goal line. As the defense are backing up, the coach shoots the puck low into the corner. The forwards are on offense and can't move until the puck is shot. It is a 2-on-2 competition with the defense trying to create a turnover and the forwards trying to score.

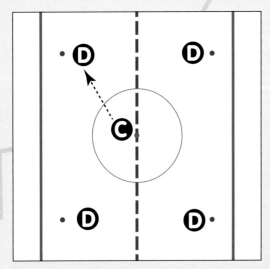

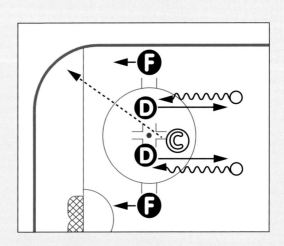

# Back Pressure

## Purpose

To apply back pressure to offensive units in a game-like situation.

## Setup

All of the players are in the neutral zone against the boards with the coach, who has the puck.

## Drill

A pair of defenders break from the boards to the blue line. They skate forward from the blue line to the red line and then backward toward the defensive zone. The coach then dumps a puck into the defensive zone. The defenders retrieve it. Simultaneously, three forwards break from the boards and join the two defenders to break out as a five-person unit.

Two new defenders break from the boards to play defense against the unit breaking out.

Three back-checking forwards are ready at the red line. As soon as their corresponding forward crosses the red line on the attack, they chase, backcheck and defend the zone.

The five-person defending unit tries to force a turnover. When they get the puck over the blue line, the coach dumps a new puck into the zone that was just cleared and the five-person defending unit breaks out on offense. A new pair of defenders jump out to defend, and three more back-checking forwards take their

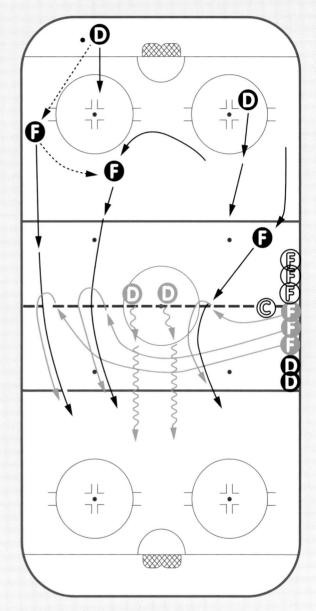

place on the red line. (In the diagram, the coach has dumped in the puck and the unit is breaking out; the defenders are ready and the back-checkers are in position, waiting for the forwards to cross the red line.)

# Neutral Zone Transition and Attack

## Purpose

To practice moving the puck in transition and into an odd-person opportunity in the offensive zone.

## Setup

The coach is on the boards at the red line with a puck. Forwards are divided into two groups (different colored jerseys or pinnies are an asset here) on the far boards inside each blue line. Defenders are divided into two groups opposite the forwards and kitty-corner to their matching colored forwards.

## Drill

A pair of defenders move to the red line and are ready to defend. Two defenders on the opposite side skate forward to the red line and backward toward their zone. The coach dumps the puck shallow into the zone behind them. One defenseman turns to get the puck and passes it to his partner (D to D).

The three forwards kitty-corner to the defenders with the puck skate toward the zone and regroup for a breakout. The defenders move the puck to the three forwards, and they attack the defending defense.

As soon as the forwards cross the blue line 3-on-2, the defenders who led the breakout stop at the red line to defend the next rush. Two new defenders (waiting on the boards in the zone where the 3-on-2 is playing out) skate forward to the red line and backward toward the blue line. The coach shallow dumps the puck into their zone, the three kitty-corner forwards move to break out, and the drill repeats nonstop.

This drill can be run 2-on-1, 3-on-1 or 3-on-2.

## Add a Double Transition

Consider this for advanced players.

In this version of the neutral zone transition and attack, when the forwards get the puck in the neutral zone from the breakout defenders, they pass the puck to the defending defenders, who pass it D to D while the forwards regroup to attack the breakout defenders. The defending defenders pass the puck to the forwards who skate towards the breakout defenders, who are now backing up to play defense. While they are still in the neutral zone, the forwards pass the puck to the breakout defenders, who pass the puck D to D while the forwards regroup again. The forwards take the pass from the break out defenders for the second time, and attack the defending defenders 3-on-2.

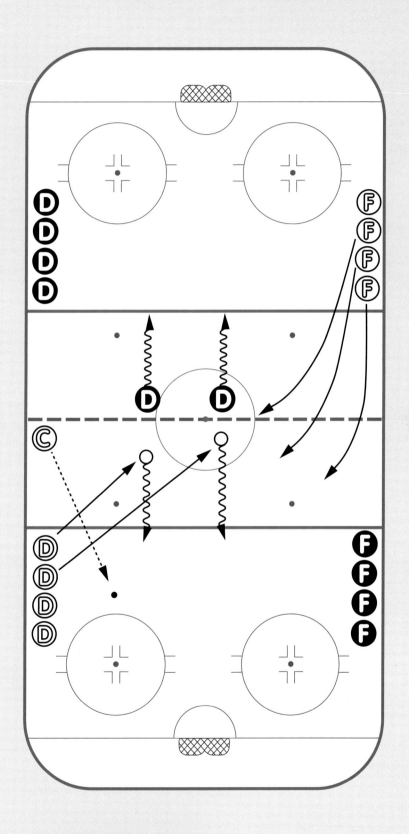

# Break Out and Defend

## Purpose

To practice moving the puck in transition to generate odd-person opportunities off the rush.

## Setup

Forwards are in the center ice circle; defense are against the boards at the hash marks. Pucks are in opposite corners.

## Drill

Two defenders start at opposite defensive zone dots. On the coach's signal, the defenders on the dots skate forward to the top of the circle, backward to the bottom of the circle and turn to retrieve a puck in the corner. At the same time, two forwards from the center circle skate into each zone and prepare to break out of the zone on the far side of the defender. The defender rims the puck around the boards toward the break out forward at the hash marks, who then passes to the second forward, who swings like a center into the zone, takes the pass and attacks at the far end. After rimming the puck, the defender skates up ice to defend against the forward who is attacking from the other end. The drill can progress to 2-on-1, 3-on-1 or 3-on-2 (with a D-to-D pass before the breakout). The initial pass can also vary. Players can rim the puck, carry the puck behind the net and pass directly to the first forward, or they can carry and pass to the second forward (center). Even more variations open up when you use two defenders. Be creative!

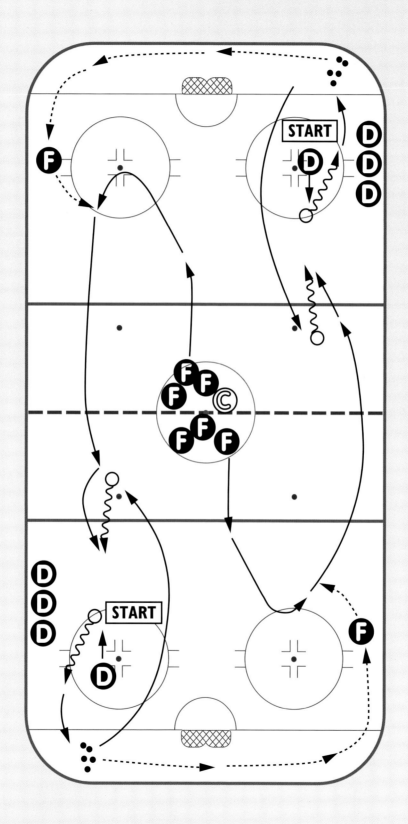

# Chip to Speed

## Purpose

As a progression of the break out and defend drill, this version lets players practice moving the puck with speed in transition to generate odd-person opportunities off the rush. It also teaches the skill of chipping a puck ahead of a moving player for an indirect pass to lead a rush.

## Setup

Same as break out and defend.

## Drill

In this progression, the forward in the center position, who receives the pass for the break out (F2 and F5), carries the puck to where the blue line meets the near boards in the defensive zone. As the player reaches this area, the coach pressures the forward, forcing a pass. This pass is the chip pass to a moving player.

F2 (and F5) chips the puck off of the boards and out of the zone to a spot ahead of F3 (or F6), where that player can retrieve it as he or she accelerates through the neutral zone. This player then attacks the defender 1-on-1. For extra fun, make the first chip earlier (i.e. half-way between the hash marks and the blue line), and add a second chip by F3 and F6 to F7 and F8 (who can come from the center circle for an offensive zone entry) for two chips in one rush. The drill can also progress to 2-on-1, 3-on-1 or 3-on-2 (with a D-to-D pass before the breakout).

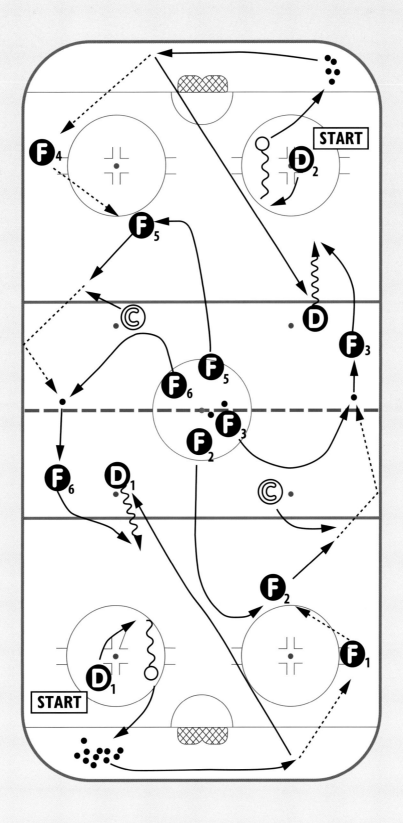

# Continuous 2-on-1

## Purpose

To practice quick puck movement in transition to generate odd-person opportunities off the rush in a continuous flow environment that encourages quick thinking and heads-up hockey with lots of opportunities for long first passes (a "quick up").

## Setup

All of the players are in the neutral zone against the boards. The coach has the puck to start.

## Drill

One defender skates forward from the blue line to the red line and then backward back to the blue line. The puck is shot behind the defender and into the zone by the coach.

Two forwards leave the neutral zone to break out of the zone with the defender. A new defender jumps into the neutral zone to defend the forwards in a 2-on-1. Two other forwards follow the first two forwards through the neutral zone and wait for a turnover forced by the defending defender. As soon as the attacking forwards get a chance on net or the defender breaks up the rush, the defending defender passes the puck as quickly as possible to one of the new forwards, who breaks out the other way. A new defender jumps into the neutral zone to defend those forwards in a 2-on-1. Two new forwards follow them through the neutral zone and the drill continues nonstop.

Defenders drive the drill, as after they defend the 2-on-1 they start the next 2-on-1. The drill can progress to 3-on-1 and 3-on-2; you can also go through the same progression with the defending defender joining the rush to add some offense!

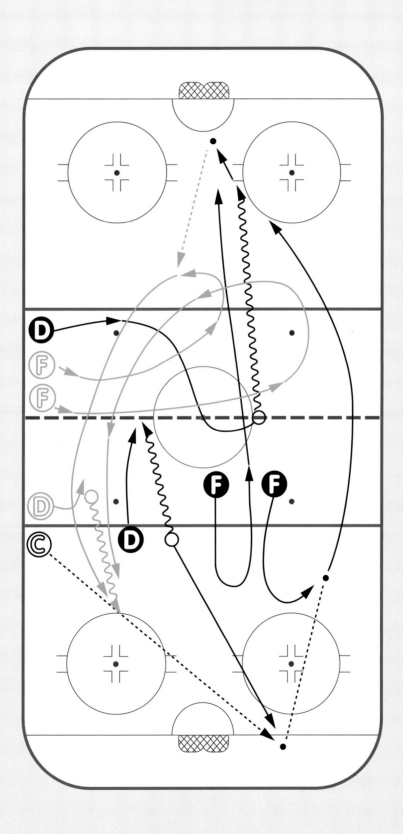

# Glossary

**BACKHAND SIDE** Opposite to your same side. Your stick blade will be away from this side of your body when you are set up in the hockey-playing position.

**BACK SKATE** The skate farthest from your target when you are shooting (or passing) in a traditional manner; the skate farthest from the object you are moving toward when doing a lateral slide.

**BALL OF THE FOOT** The somewhat circular mound at the bottom of your foot, at the base of your big toe.

**BLADE OF THE STICK SQUARE TO THE ICE** Holding or moving your stick in a position such that the greatest portion of the bottom of the blade is on the ice.

**BLADE RADIUS** The contour or profile of the blade.

**BODY SQUARE TO THE OBJECT (OR A DIRECTION)** Positioning your body such that your shoulders and upper torso are facing the object or direction.

**BOTTOM HAND** Your same-side hand, which holds the shaft of your stick below your top hand (or the top of the stick).

**BREAK(ING) YOUR WRISTS** The motion of rotating both your top and bottom hands while shooting or passing the puck so that the stick's blade moves from a closed position while holding the puck to an open position and then quickly to a closed position when releasing the puck; also very extreme rotation of your wrists.

**CENTERLINE OF THE BODY** An imaginary line dividing the body in half lengthwise, from top to bottom.

**CLOSED BLADE** For a right-handed player: the blade of your stick, starting from a position square on the ice, is rotated to create an angle to the ice of less than 90 degrees when the backhand side of your blade faces the ice and greater than 90 degrees when the forehand side of your blade faces the ice. For a left-handed player: the blade of your stick, starting from a position square on the ice, is rotated to create an angle to the ice of less than 90 degrees when the forehand side of your blade faces the ice and greater than 90 degrees when the backhand side of your blade faces the ice.

**CYCLE OF POWER** The full movement of the drive skate through one cycle during a particular skating technique.

**DRIVE** The combined force of a leg and skate pushing down toward the ice and away from the body.

**FAR SIDE** Relative to a player, the side of the net farthest from the player.

**FEET SQUARE TO THE OBJECT (OR A DIRECTION)** Positioning your feet such that your toes are facing the object or direction.

**FLAT BLADE** A "perfectly" flat skate blade—you are on a skate blade that is flat from front to back and from side to side.

**FLAT BLADE, FRONT TO BACK** Your weight is evenly distributed over the entire length of your skate blade, from the ball of your foot (front) to your heel (back).

**FLAT BLADE, SIDE TO SIDE** Your weight (and the pressure you apply) is evenly distributed over the inside and outside edges of your skate blade.

**FOREHAND SIDE** The proper side (or same side); the side opposite your off side. This is the side you shoot from when taking a forehand shot, and it is the side your stick blade will be on when you are set up in the hockey-playing position.

**FRONT SKATE** The skate closest to your target when you are shooting (or passing) in a traditional manner; the skate closest to the object you are moving toward when doing a lateral slide.

**HEEL OF THE BLADE** The bottom of the blade; the part of the blade that is closest to the connection of the blade to the shaft.

**HEEL OF THE FOOT** The pad at the bottom of your foot, at the back of your foot.

**HOCKEY-PLAYING POSITION** The basic stance for playing hockey when you have two hands on your stick.

**HOCKEY-SKATING POSITION** The basic stance for skating when you have one hand on your stick.

**HOLLOW** The concave groove between the two edges of your skate blade.

**INSIDE EDGE OF THE SKATE BLADE** The edge of the skate blade that is closest to the inside of your skate and foot (the same side as your big toe).

**LATERAL ATTACK MOVE** Any deke where you combine a lateral movement with forward motion to go around, or separate from, a player.

**LATERAL (HORIZONTAL) WEIGHT TRANSFER** Having your weight over one skate and then shifting or moving your weight so that it is over the other skate.

**MOVING TO THE OFF SIDE** Moving to the side away from the way you shoot (i.e., a right-handed player moving to the left; a left-handed player moving to the right).

**NEAR SIDE** Relative to a player, the side of the net closest to the player.

**OFF FOOT OR SKATE** The foot that is opposite to your proper (same) side (i.e., the left foot for a right-handed player; the right foot for a left-handed player).

**OFF SIDE** The side opposite your (proper) same side (i.e., the left side for a right-handed player; the right side for a left-handed player).

**OPENING THE BLADE** For a right-handed player: the blade of your stick, starting from a position square on the ice, is rotated to create an angle to the ice of less than 90 degrees when the forehand side of your blade faces the ice and greater than 90 degrees when the backhand side of your blade faces the ice. For a left-handed player: the blade of your stick, starting from a position square on the ice, is rotated to create an angle to the ice of less than 90 degrees when the backhand side of your blade faces the ice and greater than 90 degrees when the forehand side of your blade faces the ice.

**OUTSIDE EDGE OF THE BLADE** The edge of the skate blade closest to the outside of your skate and foot (the same side as your pinky toe).

**PAD OF THE FOOT** The mound or pad on the bottom of your foot that runs along the base of all your toes—from the circular mound at the base of the big toe (the ball of the foot) to the mound under the pinky toe (the metatarsal pad).

**PITCH OF THE SKATE** The angle of the bottom of the foot in the skate relative to the blade of the skate.

**PROPER SIDE** Opposite to the off side (i.e., the right side for a right-handed player; the left side for a left-handed player).

**RADIUS OF HOLLOW (ROH)** The depth of the hollow between the two edges of your skate blade.

**RECOVERY** After the drive and thrust, bringing the drive skate back to its original position to repeat the cycle of power.

**ROTATION OF THE TOP HAND** Turning the wrist of the top hand while holding the stick with the proper grip, causing the blade to open or close.

**SAME SIDE** Opposite to the off side (i.e., the right side for a right-handed player; the left side for a left-handed player).

**SAME FOOT OR SKATE** The foot that is opposite to your off side, (i.e., the right foot for a right-handed player; the left foot for a left-handed player).

**TOE OF THE STICK BLADE** The end of the stick blade, farthest from where the blade connects to the shaft.

**TOP HAND** The hand at the top of the shaft of the stick.

**TRADITIONAL SHOT/PASS** Shooting or passing with your feet facing 90 degrees to your target. Your weight is carried from your back foot (same foot) to your front foot (off foot) when on your forehand, and from the back foot (off foot) to your front foot (same foot) when on your backhand.

# Acknowledgments

I sincerely want to thank the following people, without whom this book would not have been the same:

**STEVE CAMERON**—my editor, for your countless hours and incredible patience; for your dedication in finding that perfect photograph; for all the time at the rink; and for understanding and embracing the message. You have brought this all to life! I can't thank you enough.

**LIONEL KOFFLER** and the staff at Firefly Books, as well as to designer Gareth Lind and copyeditor Nancy Foran—thank you for your expertise and for helping to turn my lessons and practice notes into a beautiful and functional book!

**RON MACLEAN** — I can't thank you enough for writing the foreword to my first edition of *Play Better Hockey*. There is no doubt that you contributed to the success of that book. Your support for the UltraSkills teaching program—throughout *Hockey Night in Canada* Hockey Days and "Think Hockey"—was appreciated so much. It has always been an absolute pleasure working with you and watching you on *Hockey Night in Canada* and *Hometown Hockey*. You have been a great ambassador right across our country for this wonderful game. Thank you for everything you have done for hockey!

**HOWIE MEEKER**—for your boundless energy and passion for teaching. It was a privilege to have you as a mentor and to work with you and your sons for over a decade. Your enthusiasm for the game was contagious. Thank you for the start you gave me.

**BOBBY SMITH**—as an NHL player you had that rare combination of elite skills and knowledge with the ability to teach. You have never lost sight of the importance of having fun on the ice. Thanks for everything you brought to UltraSkills!

**CYRIL LEEDER**—thanks for that unforgettable call in the middle of the night to tell me that you had come up with the perfect costume for "UltraMan ... Bulls-eye!" You have lived the passion with me Cy—and we have always been on the same page. Thanks for always being there for me and for everything you have done for hockey in Ottawa.

**BRIAN KILREA**—it was a pleasure to play for you coach! You taught me the most important hockey lesson: have fun every time you are on the ice. It is a lesson I have never forgotten. I had fun every practice and game with you behind the bench. Thanks for making a difference, Killer!

**NIGEL LESTER**—you were my lead instructor when I started at Howie's in 1974. We have taught together for over three decades. Thanks for everything you gave, every year, to UltraSkills.

**DAVE KONAROWSKI**—your love for skates and blades and your knowledge of the impact they have is unrivalled. Your passion hits me whenever I walk into Crow's. Don't ever lose it!

**MOM AND DAD**—for introducing me to this incredible game, for driving me to the rink a million times, for taking me to see Canada play the Soviets when I was 10 and planting the seed of my dream to play for my country—and then encouraging me to pursue that dream ... For everything that you did for so many years... I will always be grateful.

**JAMES AND JOHN** —for the hours we spent playing shinny, hoping time would stand still. For experiencing, with me, the game the way it was meant to be played, and for our never ending discussions about hockey. At the corner rink we lived the dream together—may we always...

**MY FAMILY**—I simply can't do justice to how grateful I am for everything you have done to allow me to pursue my passion. Thank you, Lynn, for your incredible support and encouragement. It has meant so much to me. You made UltraSkills possible, and *Play Better Hockey* would never have happened without your support. And to Talia, Lauren, Taryn and Sean. I can't thank you enough for sharing this passion with me. I have loved coaching you and watching you play. Remember, I am your biggest fan! May you continue to enjoy this wonderful game for many years to come!